understanding **poststructuralism**

Understanding Movements in Modern Thought
Series Editor: Jack Reynolds

This series provides short, accessible and lively introductions to the major schools, movements and traditions in philosophy and the history of ideas since the beginning of the Enlightenment. All books in the series are written for undergraduates meeting the subject for the first time.

Published

Understanding Existentialism
Jack Reynolds

Understanding Poststructuralism
James Williams

Understanding Virtue Ethics
Stan van Hooft

Forthcoming titles include

Understanding Empiricism
Robert Meyers

Understanding Ethics
Tim Chappell

Understanding Feminism
Peta Bowden and Jane Mummery

Understanding German Idealism
Will Dudley

Understanding Hegelianism
Robert Sinnerbrink

Understanding Hermeneutics
Lawrence Schmidt

Understanding Naturalism
Jack Ritchie

Understanding Phenomenology
David Cerbone

Understanding Rationalism
Charlie Heunemann

Understanding Utilitarianism
Tim Mulgan

understanding **poststructuralism**

James Williams

ACUMEN

For Richard and Olive
It is always about who you learn from.

First published in 2005 by Acumen
Reprinted in 2007

Acumen Publishing Limited
Stocksfield Hall
Stocksfield
NE43 7TN
www.acumenpublishing.co.uk

ISBN 978-1-84465-032-3 (hardcover)
ISBN 978-1-84465-033-0 (paperback)

Work on Chapter 3 was supported by  Arts & Humanities
Research Council

British Library Cataloguing-in-Publication Data
A catalogue record for this book is available from the British Library.

Designed and typeset in Garamond by Kate Williams, Swansea.
Printed and bound in Malta by Gutenberg Press.

Contents

Acknowledgements

I should like to thank The Carnegie Trust for the Universities of Scotland for its generous funding for research in Paris libraries. La Bibliothèque du Saulchoir, Paris, provided a stimulating research environment and a wonderful research resource. Work on Chapter 3 was supported by the Arts and Humanities Research Council. Material from Chapter 3 was presented at the Experimenting with Intensities Conference (May 2004) at Trent University, Canada, with travel funded by the British Academy, and at the Writing/History: Deleuzian Events Conference (June 2005) at the University of Cologne. Chapter 4 was presented in part at the Department of Political Science, Carleton University, Canada. I am grateful for their support and very useful feedback. Chapter 1 was presented at the Graduate Visiting Speaker Series, Department of English Literature, University of Edinburgh. Parts of this book were also presented at the Research Seminar in the Philosophy Department, University of Dundee. The University of Dundee funded sabbatical leave for this project. Kurt Brandhorst, Claire Colebrook, Nicholas Davey, John Drummond, Penny Fielding, Lily Forrester, Rachel Jones, Beth Lord, Valentine Moulard, Aislinn O'Donnell, Keith Ansell Pearson, John Protevi, Dan Smith, Michael Wheeler, Frédéric Worms and many others challenged and helped me in conversations and through their research. At Acumen Steven Gerrard, Tristan Palmer and Kate Williams made this a much better book through their careful editorial advice. My undergraduate and postgraduate classes and tutees gave me the opportunity to try out many parts of this work in a sympathetic but critical environment. They prompted ideas in ways that can never be traced fully, but that are the lifeblood of academic work. I am grateful to all friends, students and colleagues for their comments and help, but claim all errors and imprecision as mine all mine.

A work owes more than could ever be quantified to the time, love and spaces that others make for it, should anyone be foolish or crude enough to try. In all of these, my immeasurable debts are to you, Claire.

Abbreviations

AK   Foucault, *The Archaeology of Knowledge* (London: Routledge, 1989).

D   Derrida, "Différance", in *Margins of Philosophy*, A. Bass (trans.), 1–28 (Chicago, IL: University of Chicago Press, 1984).

DR   Deleuze, *Difference and Repetition*, P. Patton (trans.) (New York: Columbia University Press, 1995).

DF   Lyotard, *Discours, figure* (Paris: Klincksieck, 1971).

HRS   Deleuze, "How do we Recognize Structuralism", in *Desert Islands and Other Texts (1953–1974)*, M. Taormina (trans.), 170–92 (New York: Semiotext(e), 2003).

OG   Derrida, *Of Grammatology*, G. C. Spivak (trans.) (Baltimore, MD: Johns Hopkins University Press, 1974).

PS   Deleuze, *Proust and Signs*, R. Howard (trans.) (London: Continuum, 2000).

RPL   Kristeva, *Revolution in Poetic Language*, M. Waller (trans.) (New York: Columbia University Press, 1984).

TD   Lyotard, *The Differend: Phrases in Dispute* (Minneapolis, MN: University of Minnesota Press, 1988).

WPU   Deleuze, "What Prisoners want from Us", in *Desert Islands and Other Texts (1953–1974)*, M. Taormina (trans.), 204–5 (New York: Semiotext(e), 2003).

one

Introduction: what is poststructuralism?

Limits and knowledge

Poststructuralism is the name for a movement in philosophy that began in the 1960s. It remains an influence not only in philosophy, but also in a wider set of subjects, including literature, politics, art, cultural criticisms, history and sociology. This influence is controversial because poststructuralism is often seen as a dissenting position, for example, with respect to the sciences and to established moral values.

The movement is best summed up by its component thinkers. Therefore, this book seeks to explain it through a critical study of five of the most important works by five of the movement's most important thinkers (Derrida, Deleuze, Lyotard, Foucault and Kristeva). The principle aim is to respond to two powerful criticisms of poststructuralism: first, that it is wilfully and irretrievably difficult; secondly, that it takes on positions that are marginal, inconsistent and impossible to maintain.

The first idea that allows for an answer to these points is that *the limits of knowledge play an unavoidable role at its core*. This is the common thread running through poststructuralism. It explains why structuralism had to be added to, since the structuralist project can be summed up as arriving at secure knowledge through the charting of differences within structures. According to poststructuralists, this security missed the troubling and productive roles of limits folded back into the structure. Knowledge cannot escape its limits: "It is not surrounded, but traversed by its limit, marked in its inside by the multiple furrows of its margin" (D: 25.)

So "limit" is not used in a specialist sense here, for example, in mathematical terms, or as the upper or lower limits of measurable quantities. Instead, it indicates relative security and stability within a given environment, where the boundaries are seen as less dependable than the centre. For poststructuralism, the core is not more reliable, significant and better known than its limits or outer boundaries. This is because the clear distinction of core and limit is not possible. The criticism of this distinction takes poststructuralism well beyond structuralist views, even though the former owes much to the latter.

Structuralist knowledge is open to change when the observed structures change. However, despite this openness to change, in noting a repeated pattern of signs the structuralist scientist hopes to arrive at some secure understanding. For example, in charting the repeated patterns of daily life (wake–work–eat–sleep) we can begin to understand the relations between each element (their order and place). There could be limits to such patterns (sleep–sleep–play–sleep) but these would be exceptional moves away from a normal pattern. The idea is that knowledge should start with the norm and only then consider the exception. The norm implies a deviation in the definition of the exception. If there is an ethical and political side to this distinction, it is that truth and the good are in the norm, although many disagreements are possible as to what makes the norm.

Poststructuralism folds the limit back on to the core of knowledge and on to our settled understanding of the true and the good. It does this in a very radical way. That is, the limit is not compared with the core, or balanced with it, or given some kind of tempering role, in the sense, for example, of a majority listening to minorities. Rather, the claim is that *the limit is the core*.

What does this strange claim mean? It means that any settled form of knowledge or moral good is made by its limits and cannot be defined independently of them. It means also that any exclusion of these limits is impossible. Limits are the truth of the core and any truths that deny this are illusory or false. The truth of a population is where it is changing. The truth of a nation is at its borders. The truth of the mind is in its limit cases. But is the definition of a limit not dependent on the notion of a prior core? You only know that sleep–sleep–sleep–drink is deviant because of the dominance of wake–work–eat–sleep. No; the autonomous definition of the limit is the next most important common thread in poststructuralism. *The limit is not defined in opposition to the core; it is a positive thing in its own right.*

This definition is radical since it calls into question the role of traditional forms of knowledge in setting definitions. No poststructuralist defines the limit as something knowable (it would then merely become another core). Rather, each poststructuralist thinker defines the limit as a version of a pure difference, in the sense of something that defies identification. The exact terminology chosen for this difference varies greatly and is very controversial. We shall see that it also raises many serious problems. So, less controversially, *the limit is an ungraspable thing that can only be approached through its function of disruption and change in the core*. You cannot identify the limit, but you can trace its effects.

Poststructuralists trace the effects of a limit defined as difference. Here, "difference" is not understood in the structuralist sense of difference between identifiable things, but in the sense of open variations (these are sometimes called processes of differentiation, at other times, pure differences). These effects are transformations, changes, revaluations. The work of the limit is to open up the core and to change our sense of its role as stable truth and value. What if life took on different patterns? What if our settled truths were otherwise? How can we make things different?

This definition of the limit as something open and ungraspable – except through its traces or expressions in more fixed forms of knowledge – leads to great variations between poststructuralists. They observe the effects in different places and follow different traces. They give different temporary and necessarily illusory characterizations of the limit.

Each of the great poststructuralist texts studied here gives a different account of the play of the limit at the core, but all share the definitions given above. Each text will have a chapter to itself where its main arguments and distinguishing features will be studied. Put simply, Derrida follows the play of the limit at the apparently more immediate and truthful core of language. Lyotard traces the effect of limit-events in language and sensation. Deleuze affirms the value of a productive limit between actual identities and virtual pure differences. Foucault traces the genealogy of the limit as the historical constitution of later tensions and problems. Kristeva follows the limit as an unconscious at work undoing and remaking linguistic structures and oppositions.

Together, these works show poststructuralism as a thorough disruption of our secure sense of meaning and reference in language, of our understanding of our senses and of the arts, of our understanding of identity, of our sense of history and of its role in the present, and of our understanding of language as something free of the work of the unconscious.

Disruption should not be seen as a negative word. One aspect of poststructuralism is its power to resist and work against settled truths and oppositions. It can help in struggles against discrimination on the basis of sex or gender, against inclusions and exclusions on the basis of race, background, class or wealth. It guards against the sometimes overt, sometimes hidden, violence of established values such as an established morality, an artistic cannon or a fixed legal framework. We shall see that this does not mean that it denies them; rather, it works within them for the better.

In each of the great works to be read here, we find specific struggles and forms of resistance. Poststructuralist works cannot be abstract theoretical reflections, since they can only show the work of the limits in the practical applications of core knowledge. They must take a given actual structure and deconstruct it, transform it, show its exclusions. Thereby, they overturn assumptions about purity (in morals), about essences (in terms of race, gender and backgrounds), about values (in art and politics), about truth (in law and philosophy).

For poststructuralism, disruption must also be seen as a positive word. It is not only that there is a work against a settled core. It is rather that there is an affirmation of the power of the limit as a source of never-ending production of new and worthwhile transformations and differences. *Poststructuralism is not against this and for that – once and for all. It is for the affirmation of an inexhaustible productive power of limits. It is for the resulting positive disruption of settled oppositions.*

Critical counters

The radical nature of poststructuralism means that it is also very controversial. There have been many attacks on the movement. In return, it has had powerful critical roles to play. These arguments and controversies have taken many forms, from accusations about the destructive nature of radical opposition to tradition, to accusations of a betrayal of the radical cause.

When making sense of the great range of often quite ignorant and vitriolic debates that have followed the spread of poststructuralism, it is helpful to look at very pure philosophical criticisms of its general form. The radical folding back of a limit, defined as pure difference, on to a core of knowledge, falls prey to the following related objections:

1. A limit must be defined in terms of a known core that takes precedence over it. After all, what is the limit a limit of?
2. It makes no sense to speak of a pure difference, since in order to

do so we must treat it as something knowable. You have to identify something in order to be able to speak of it.

3. Truth is a matter of consistency and therefore presupposes some kind of core, if only in terms of logic.
4. To deny a core is to fall into relativism, where all values are relative. If all claims are relative to different values, how do we choose justly between different claims? How do we deny extreme values?
5. Moral goods depend on a core, and relativism is therefore to abandon morality. Many of our most important values are not relative.

These objections have great intuitive strength. They capture common-sense intuitions about the nature of truth and morality. They also sum up apparently straightforward arguments about the links between knowledge, justice and morality. This common-sense background has led debates to be rather simple and polarized, as if we need to take one side or the other dependent on whether we really care about truth, logic and morality.

The simplicity is illusory and very damaging, however, since it fails to register that all the great poststructuralist works to be read here develop their arguments with a strong critical awareness of these points. Their answers to the points could begin to be summed up as follows:

1. There is no known core that does not presuppose the limit. The limit comes first, not the core.
2. Sense is something more than knowledge. There are important things that matter exactly because we cannot identify them.
3. There is truth as consistency, but there is a deeper truth as variation (the truth of the radically new as opposed to the truth of the settled).
4. To deny absolutes, such as a certain core, is not to deny significant differences that we can act upon.
5. There is an ethics associated with showing that a core hides differences and suppresses them; this is not to deny morality, but to deny that ethics is a matter of absolutes.

These answers show that the critical arguments must be taken a step higher. The real critical issues for the defence of poststructuralism are whether it can be shown on a case by case basis that:

- A core is destabilized by its limits.
- This destabilization is ethically positive.

- It involves a new sense of truth beyond identity in reference and coherence in structure.
- Showing something in practice is as valuable as demonstrating it once and for all.

In other words, the goal is not to give final answers to the criticisms. It is to show that they do not apply in practical but far-reaching cases (sometimes so far-reaching that they can appear to be new claims to universal truths).

This leads to an important further definition. *Poststructuralism is a practice.* It is not about abstract arguments or detached observations, but about a practical expression of the limits in a given core. This explains why different varieties of poststructuralism are given names that correspond to practical critical and creative activities: deconstruction (Derrida), libidinal economics (Lyotard), genealogy and archaeology (Foucault), transcendental empiricism (Deleuze), dialectics (Deleuze, Kristeva).

This pragmatic side to poststructuralism invites further critical arguments, since it seems to commit it to endless critical and constructive work, with no final truths in sight. This is indeed the case. There is an irresolvable difference between the poststructuralist commitment to practice and any commitment to an absolute foundation or final end in knowledge, logic or morality. *Poststructuralism is constantly revived through openness to the new (to pure difference). It is opposed to any absolute certainty, but can only work through this opposition in repeated critical and creative practices.*

This series of arguments and oppositions is not merely theoretical. The philosophical arguments have consequences and parallels in familiar political and moral disputes. If the left in politics is defined as a politics for the margins, for those who are excluded and for those who are defined as inferior and kept there, then *poststructuralism is a politics of the left.* If the right in politics is defined as a politics of fixed truths and values, whether these are fixed traditions, or inalienable values, or eternal moral truths, then poststructuralism is opposed to such a politics. It also draws fire and distaste from the right. This critique has often been vitriolic and deeply ill-informed.

However, given these definitions, it is a mistake to identify particular political parties or movements with the right and with the left. If a particular margin is valued, once and for all, then it cannot fit the definition of the left set out here. So a politics that rests on particular values, once and for all, is of the right; this is independent of how "good" those values are judged to be at a given time. This does not mean that poststructuralism, defined as a politics of the left, cannot fight for causes. It means that the reason for fighting for those causes has to be because they are right at a particular time and given a particular situation, rather than because the causes are cases of a wider absolute and eternal good. The struggle is for these rights now and not for universal *and* eternal rights.

This also means that the poststructuralist political struggle cannot appeal to absolutes and must seek to undermine them as they begin to appear, even in a politics that poststructuralists favour. So, as a politics of the left, poststructuralism cannot depend on certainty and unchangeable convictions. This does not mean that it cannot act; on the contrary, that kind of certainty is often a weakness or a lie, or a form of self-delusion. Conviction should be open to change; it should seek to change. Where it fails to do this, there is no thought.

Each of the poststructuralists considered here took stands on key injustices and conflicts. Derrida has written powerfully against apartheid. Lyotard militated for the Algerian struggles for independence and revolution, as well as the May 1968 student uprisings in his own university. Foucault and Deleuze campaigned for better conditions in prisons. Kristeva is an important figure in contemporary feminism. *The turn away from absolutes in poststructuralism has not hindered political action; it has given it a different form.*

Philosophical roots: Husserl and Heidegger

Although it is associated with works produced in the 1960s and 1970s, poststructuralism has deep historical roots. These allow for a better sense of the meaning and possibility of folding limits back. They also allow for a better understanding of why poststructuralism allows for this definition of its practice. *Poststructuralism is a heavily historical movement reacting to a long series of philosophical ideas. It is also, though, a revolutionary way of thinking about history.*

It is possible to see these philosophical roots in terms of which ones are being reacted to and which borrowed from, but this does not allow for a subtle enough understanding. This is because all the main figures in this history have provided positive and negative influences. It is also because poststructuralism continues to alter its roots. The past changes in the present and roots are not foundations. So it is better to look at the detail of which ideas have been picked up and transformed, rather than catalogue continuities and oppositions. Poststructuralism can therefore be seen as a series of interpretations of its historical roots. Each interpretation of these influences is also a transformation. So it makes more sense to think of the roots in terms of what they made possible and how they defined a terrain, rather than specific elements that were either repudiated or kept. It is a mistake to think of the movement as simply "Kantian" or simply "Anti-Cartesian", for example.

The roots that will be covered here are among the most obvious and shared ones, but there will necessarily be exclusions that can only be justified as resulting from lack of space and time, rather than any careful principle. We shall cover the following movements and thinkers in turn: phenomenology and Husserl; hermeneutics and Heidegger; psychoanalysis and Freud; transcendental philosophy and Kant; and existentialism and Nietzsche. It should not be inferred from this list that the thinkers are clear-cut representatives of the movements.

If phenomenology is defined (no doubt overly simply) as the study of how consciousness is directed or intends towards things, and as the search for the truth or essence of that intentionality, then poststructuralism involves a critique of such truth or essences. The phenomenologist method of seeking to cut away to, or perform a reduction to an inner essence does not arrive at certainty.

For example, poststructuralist philosophers have sought to show how innate senses of our own consciousness and its relation to things cannot be separated from much wider contexts. When I think that my inner sense of hearing my own voice is somehow more certain than hearing those of others, I miss the social conditioning and external causes at work in that inner sense. This is also true of other sensations and forms of self-consciousness or inner sense. Such forms of "presence" – to use Derrida's term – cannot be separated from their external limits in language, social experiences and forms of knowledge. *There is no pure presence.*

However, phenomenological methods are not thereby rejected by poststructuralism. They are rejected as the only way to truth or essence, but they are important for understanding the hold that intentionality and subjectivity have on us. They are also important for arriving at starting-points for a dilution, or undoing, or transforming extension, of our ideas of the self, of the subject and of consciousness. *Poststructuralism does not simply reject things. It works within them to undo their exclusive claims to truth and purity.*

So it is not that poststructuralists reject the self, the subject, the "I" or intersubjectivity, as some have claimed. Rather it is that these must be seen as taking place in wider historical, linguistic and experiential contexts. It is not so much that there is no "I", it is that it cannot claim to be an independent secure core. Other subjects, language beyond our control, and experiences that sunder our senses, operate within our most intimate perceptions and intuitions.

For poststructuralism, it is important to trace how what lies beyond the boundaries of the subject, consciousness and the self still operates within those boundaries (for example, in terms of ethical relations, how others maintain a hold on the self). In studying and working with phenomenology, poststructuralists are able to connect to this powerful source of an apparently secure core. They are able to work against that power, not with the aim of having done with it, but in order to bring wider interactions to our attention.

This extension and transformation of phenomenology was already underway in the work of Martin Heidegger. He added a hermeneutic element to phenomenology by showing that past meanings in language could not be abstracted from any given existence (or being). Herme-neutics, as the interpretation of the past in terms of transformations and debts, must be part of any current truths. Metaphysics, or philo-sophical systems, are not only necessarily historical in their relations to one another, they are also necessarily part of everyday existence and language.

If there was to be an idea of existence that held true beyond these ideas of historical unfolding, it was in terms of more authentic or fundamental relations to our existence (*Dasein* or there-being) and of what allowed all things to appear as beings (Being). It was not that authenticity or the fundamental could be treated as separate from the history of beings, metaphysics and knowledge. Rather, their truth had to be thought alongside historical truths. In this sense, the authentic and the fundamental were the limits to be folded back on the historical.

For example, although a human life can be thought of in many different ways, in terms of its personal history, scientific studies of it, its character and beliefs, Heidegger views its essence or authenticity as being-towards-death. We do not have to be aware of this, or to think about it, for being-towards-death to be our deeper truth. It pervades all other ways about thinking about the life and sheds a more truthful light on them. In that sense, being-towards-death is the limit that must be folded back on to other apparently more secure ways of thinking about life.

It could be inferred from this that Heidegger should be called a poststructuralist. This is a tempting idea, despite the historical prob-lem of situating his work, beginning early in the twentieth century, with poststructuralism, beginning in the 1960s. The idea should be resisted for two reasons. First, Heidegger's philosophy has never been adopted straightforwardly by poststructuralists. His work on metaphysics and truth, his distinctions drawn between beings and Being and his move away from the subject towards the starker *Dasein* or "there-being" have all been very influential in poststructuralist works, but they have been replaced by related yet different terms. For example, although Derrida has been profoundly influenced by Heidegger, he replaces the Heideggerian practice and term of destruction with deconstruction.

Secondly, it can be argued that Heidegger still retains a strong characterization of the limit in terms of authenticity. This lies in contrast with the much more open ideas of pure difference found in poststructuralism. This is a crucial difference in reflecting on the relation between Heidegger's philosophy and his overt support for the Nazi party for a period leading up to the Second World War. This relation between fascism and Heidegger's philosophy has been reacted to strongly in poststructuralist works (in Derrida and Lyotard, for instance). Part of this reaction is in response to the accusation that there are parallel political risks in poststructuralism, owing to either a perceived relativism or an opposition to essential human values.

Philosophical roots: Freud, Kant and Nietzsche

Freud's work has a much less ambiguous place in the roots of poststructuralism than Heidegger's. This is because Freud's work on the unconscious is an important stage towards poststructuralism, but it is reacted to very strongly and transformed. In fact, other psychoanalysts, such as Jacques Lacan, are adopted more straightforwardly than Freud, although not by all and, again, not without transformations.

A simple explanation for the interest but also wariness with respect to Freud is that he provides much of the conceptual framework for the understanding of the importance of the unconscious by poststructuralism, but he also stands for a mistaken orthodoxy on the content and form of the unconscious. In short, *for poststructuralism, there is an unconscious. It matters for any understanding of consciousness, but it does not follow the detail of Freud's account*, notably with respect to infantile sexuality, in castration anxiety, for instance.

Freud's description of unconscious drives is very important for many poststructuralist thinkers. For example, they owe much to the distinction drawn between a pleasure principle (we are driven to seek the pleasure associated with the diminution of an intense sensation) and a death drive (we are also driven to seek the excitations associated with destructive increases in intensity). However, they criticize Freud when these drives are explained in terms of normal states associated with gender or sexuality, since this contravenes the openness and variability found in many poststructuralist thinkers. There is no fixed "natural" state, either for the unconscious, or for its relation to consciousness and to actual behaviour.

This distinction means that poststructuralist thinkers cannot be seen as adopting the specifics of Freudian therapy, for example, in terms of the interpretations of dreams. Neither can poststructuralists be taken as following any strongly deterministic interpretation of the relation between the unconscious and conscious acts or neuroses. The whole point of the idea of the limit, and of the many different poststructuralist interpretations of it, is its resistance to systematization in terms of content or identity, or in terms of its causal relation to the core.

Because of this commitment to openness and to a resistance to the definition of limits in terms of identity, *poststructuralists are opposed to all forms of essentialism, determinism and naturalism*. For example, in reaction to Freud's work on the unconscious, it makes no sense to speak of naturally determined sexuality or deviancy from a natural norm (whether evolved or essential).

The common accusation against Freud that his views of the unconscious and his therapy do not have a scientific basis does not, therefore, apply to poststructuralism, since it is not making scientific claims about the unconscious or for a fixed psychoanalytic practice. This does not mean that the relation between poststructuralism and science is a simple one. It will be covered in greater depth in many of the following chapters, since it is crucial for many of the debates around the value of poststructuralism.

Two important questions arise at this point: the first is about philosophical method; the second about philosophical goals. If poststructuralism is not making scientific claims (whether empirical or rational) then what is the methodological basis for its views on the unconscious and on the role of limits? If poststructuralism is resistant to all forms of determinism, to norms and to specific goals, then what is its positive point?

These questions can be put in different terms that explain the importance of Kant for poststructuralism. What are the grounds for claims to truth in poststructuralism? Have poststructuralist thinkers abandoned the great philosophical tradition of the Enlightenment? Is poststructuralism a new form of dogmatism? Have poststructuralist thinkers abandoned all hope in reforming and bettering the world; have they hence fallen into nihilism?

Responses to these questions lead to an ambivalent relation to Kant. First, poststructuralism owes much to the Kantian method of transcendental philosophy. This philosophical method searches for the necessary conditions for a given intuition. These conditions are not causes; this explains the break with causal determinism. Instead, these conditions provide the necessary grounds and formal laws for intuitions, thereby resisting claims to relativism, dogmatism and nihilism. Transcendental philosophy deduces the necessary frame for things to appear as they do.

In poststructuralism, the limits can be seen as the transcendental conditions for the core. This does not mean that the limits cause the core, hence leading them to be overly determined, in the sense of being objects of knowledge like any others. The limits are not subject to causal laws. They are not part of chains of causes and effects. Instead, they are like causal laws, rather than actual causes, in standing outside the things they apply to. They give the form for something rather than having an effect on it.

This means that the deduced limits provide a formal legislating framework for the core. That is, they lead to laws or principles that apply to knowledge and that change our common view of what is known. Poststructuralism is about deducing limit-principles implied by given events; for example, in the deduction of principles that counter claims that the core is pure, or final, or absolute. However, the nature of principles is heavily altered, because principles become much more flexible and open to change. Principles become part of an experimental practice, rather than an external guide for it.

Poststructuralists cannot adopt Kant's transcendental philosophy unchanged, since it leads to exactly the kind of conditions that they seek to reject, for example, in terms of universal ethical laws, or in terms of fixed categories for the understanding. Kant's transcendental philosophy goes too far in fixing the conditions for given things or intuitions. The problem is, though, can poststructuralist thinkers resist Kant's conclusions while adopting his method?

Secondly, poststructuralists want to maintain the progressive nature of Kant's enlightenment; that is, it is worth struggling for some good guided by thought. However, poststructuralists resist Kant's specific understanding of thought as reason and of the goals of enlightenment as human freedom within carefully defined legal frameworks. We should think and act for a better world, but not with a Kantian definition of reason or with his goal of a cosmopolitan world brought together under the banner of humanism.

Poststructuralism is not a form of anti-humanism or irrationalism. It is a practice that attempts to show the limits and problems of humanism and rationalism while maintaining their progressive drive. The ambivalent roots of poststructuralism in Kant lead it to redefine the conditions of thought away from human reason and towards much wider bodily, systematic and structural processes. In turn, these processes are thought of in terms of the conditions for their changes and evolutions, rather than as fixed and closed entities.

This ambivalence also leads poststructuralism to redefine the conditions of action away from freedom (defined as the condition for non-externally caused actions of a human subject) and towards openness (defined as the condition for radical novelty within well-determined systems and structures). Instead of reason, there are thought processes. Instead of freedom, there is openness. Reason and freedom are not discarded, but set against a wider background.

This ambivalence and its consequences are not new. Questions about anti-humanism and irrationalism had been raised against Nietzsche long before the advent of poststructuralism. The form of his responses and of his critical attacks on the Kantian and Platonic legacies are very important for the development of poststructuralist thought. Three key areas of his philosophy stand out for their influence on poststructuralism:

- his genealogical method, as a critique of all forms of transcendence;
- his emphasis on the importance of style for thought;
- his search for a new way of thinking about the metaphysical basis of philosophy.

Nietzsche's philosophy allows for a better understanding of the practice of poststructuralism as something that works critically from within a situation, rather than by positing something outside it. This is because Nietzsche attacks all transcendent values that claim an independence from the historical struggles and valuations that give rise to them.

It is important to distinguish "transcendent" and "transcendental". A transcendent realm is external, superior and independent. It sets superior values that can then be applied to a lower realm. It is like a different world that gives ours direction, while maintaining its independence (a godly realm, for example). A transcendental condition is internal, different but not superior, and dependent on the given intuition it is deduced from. It gives the form for those intuitions, but sets no external values. It is a different but entirely dependent part of our world.

For Nietzsche, everything has a historical genealogy. Everything has evolved through historical struggles and everything continues to evolve. Nothing is independent of its genealogy and all genealogies intertwine. Therefore, all things are part of the same realm, that is, they are all immanent, rather than some being transcendent. This is one of his strongest legacies to poststructuralist thinkers. *For poststructuralism, values are necessarily immanent and abstract external truths are illusions.*

An important consequence of this commitment to immanence is that the realm within which all things occur – the realm within which everything is immanent – cannot itself be perfectly well ordered. It cannot have a well-defined centre and periphery, or a fixed order of measures and priorities. This is because such a system of ordering or measurement would be transcendent to the world it applied to. Instead, the realm varies according to relative perspectives of different actors and thinkers. *For poststructuralism, truth becomes a matter of perspective rather than absolute order.*

This means that style, as innovating expression of individual perspective, becomes very important because it comes to replace universals truths and forms of rationality. This is not style in the sense of different ways of doing something, as in different schools of painting, for example. It is style in the sense of an expression of individuality.

Style is what sets an individual apart. It must always be something new, mobile and distinctive, in order to resist settled measures and orders. It must also be something that communicates individuality without lending an absolute transparency to it, since this would be to fall back into the illusion of perfect communication and universally accessible truths.

This has two results in poststructuralist works. First, *poststructuralist thinkers tend to experiment with style in terms of writing and methods.* This does not necessarily mean that they are examples of "good" style or "stylishness" in some well-defined sense. On the contrary, the demand for innovation and for communication as individual expression often makes postmodern works extremely difficult, although also very rewarding and enticing.

Secondly, style in poststructuralist works is deliberately resistant to perfect understanding and deliberately demanding of different reactions depending on perspective. *Poststructuralist works invite varieties of different interpretations and resist single final and universally communicable meanings.*

Nietzsche's doctrine of will to power (everything is will to power and nothing else) provides an example of the kind of explanations needed to justify claims about multiple perspectives, about the necessity of genealogy and about the absence of any transcendent values. All things are ongoing processes, as struggles between different wills to power, between different values, different ways of life, and between different forms of life. No ideas can stand outside these struggles.

Many poststructuralists follow Nietzsche's explanation in order either to provide a metaphysics to underlie their broader philosophical claims (Deleuze, Lyotard, Foucault) or to begin to outline new concepts capable of accounting for differences resistant to identification and oppositions (Derrida, Kristeva).

A key series of questions returned to throughout Nietzschean interpretations therefore plagues poststructuralism. What is the status of explanations of the processes of will to power and of pure difference? Do they involve ultimate claims about the nature of all things? Or are they speculations and fictions, designed to prompt thought but not to make final claims to truth? If poststructuralists are making such final claims, does that not contradict their views on the limits of knowledge? If they are not making such claims, are they not just putting forward fanciful theories that should be given no more credence than science fiction?

Science, art and value

Scientific theories and the more detailed discoveries and data from empirical science now dominate our views of ourselves and of the world. They also play the main role in setting out the situations we need to react to and how we can react to them. As answered by the sciences, the questions "What are the facts?" and "How can we forecast how things will turn out?" guide our acts towards the future, for example, in terms of deciding on the use of energy resources or in reacting to new viruses.

Yet, despite this dominance, poststructuralism is not primarily focused on the model of science in terms of the understanding and guidance of thought. Instead, this model is criticized and reflected upon, even sometimes ignored in favour of more aesthetic models. *For poststructuralism, the dominance of the model of the sciences and of scientific knowledge should be resisted.*

These remarks raise a series of serious critical remarks against poststructuralism. First, in terms of method:

- Is it not the case that science provides the paradigm for methods, in terms of the discovery and rejection of truths and the construction of theories?
- Should poststructuralist theories not be falsifiable through counter-evidence, in the same way as scientific theories?
- Should they also not be subject to the same demands of consistency as scientific theories?

Secondly, in terms of content:

- Is it not the case that science, rather than art, provides the data that we must use for understanding the world?
- Should poststructuralism not follow the latest scientific discoveries and use them as the proper basis for reflection?
- Is it not a mistake to take outdated or non-empirical views of the world, as a basis for action?

In short, the accusation is that, by ignoring scientific discoveries, post-structuralism peddles a false view of the world. It is also that, by ignoring scientific method, it puts forward theories that are not subject to the possibility of being constructed on the basis of evidence or proved false by it.

Answers to these important critical questions begin with the remark that poststructuralists are aware of the dominance of scientific theories, discoveries and methods. However, they are critical of this dominance because they define thought as a process that runs with, but also independently of science. On this view, thought is at the limit of science and goes beyond it, allowing for a more profound perspective on it.

In poststructuralism, life is not to be defined solely by science, but by the layers of history and future creations captured in wider senses of language, thought and experience. This explains why poststructuralists do not seem to spend that much time on the sciences. In fact, *when they resist and criticize attempts to give a scientific view of language, poststructuralists are making a wider point about science and its limits.* Furthermore, the future of thought cannot be guided solely by science. Our desires, acts and thoughts have valuable extra-scientific dimensions. These dimensions are an important part of a full sense of life. Science cannot operate independently of that part and does not do so even when it claims to. Many poststructuralist arguments are reactions to the technological approach to life characterized by science (when done in abstraction or without imagination). They stress undervalued and hidden influences at work within science.

In order to advance these arguments, poststructuralist texts cannot restrict themselves to a scientific view or methodology. Instead, they approach other texts with relations to science, such as works from the history of philosophy, works of art and works of literature. The point is to show that there are truths resistant to scientific methodology and truths different from scientific facts. These truths have a role to play in relation to science, for example, through a critique of technological approaches to the world or through alternatives to the logic of scientific methods.

Poststructuralists are not anti-science or anti-technology; rather, they see important dimensions that cannot be accounted for from within science. Unlike similar positions, though, poststructuralism does not advocate realms that are completely separate from science, as if there were a realm for science and a realm for ethics or aesthetics, for example. Instead, the critical point that the limits of knowledge are at its core is applied to scientific theories and to theories about scientific methodology. Science cannot justify claims to objectivity or to greatest truthfulness, since the grounds for such claims are themselves open to critique or to deconstruction in terms of their limits. There is no purely scientific ground for the justification of science.

Scientific theories and facts must therefore be seen as part of a much wider series of extra-scientific theories and criticisms, in particular, in terms of the impossibility of final theories or final truths. The assumption that science is the main arbiter of fact and the main paradigm for method comes under scrutiny with poststructuralism in terms of its presuppositions and exclusions. Here, "extra-scientific" must be understood as beyond the limits of restricted definitions of science in terms of method, in terms of relations to truths, and in terms of forms of evidence and logic. It is quite possible to define poststructuralism as empirical, but where experimentation is not given any predetermined limits. This point is important, since otherwise the claim to something "extra-scientific" would contradict the thoroughgoing poststructuralist critique of fixed oppositions and limits.

In poststructuralism, the assumption that scientific method is somehow pure or objective is contrasted with values still at work in that assumption. For example, the language of science and the forms used to justify it are analysed for false presuppositions, with respect to time, space and reality (Deleuze), with respect to narratives of progress (Lyotard), with respect to ethical or epistemological neutrality (Foucault, Kristeva) or with respect to freedom from implied metaphysics (Derrida). This extension into value does not imply a rejection of science at all. It implies a rejection of the dominance of science, or perhaps more accurately of a certain and possibly false image of science, especially where it becomes either an arbiter of value (for example, in terms of morality) or where it is claimed to be value free (for example, in terms of being able to give value-neutral determinations of human and animal essences or life).

The attraction of art for poststructuralism is therefore in the way art opens on to different senses of value. It does so through the complexity of art, that is, through the way it allows for multiple interpretations and creative responses. It also does so by exhibiting the way in which value is created rather than essential, pre-given, or explicable through natural evolution.

Art provides material for practical thinking on the relation of different kinds of knowledge to the disruptive power of their limits (Foucault gives historical examples of this in painting and architecture, for instance). The rich variety of ideas and sensations found in a single artwork go beyond scientific understanding both of the work and of its ideal and emotional contents.

Artworks involve forms of experience that show the limits of established ways of understanding and of valuing environments and experiences (Lyotard and Deleuze are interested in this in painting and film, for example, with respect to experiences of space, time and memory). Art's relation to the unconscious shows the limits of consciousness and of the self (in the work of Kristeva). Works of art show how meaning is always excessive and resistant to final patterns or methods of interpretation (Derrida's deconstructions work through this).

Poststructuralism goes beyond art-criticism or theories of art to become part of artistic processes. In poststructuralism, there are no external valuations of what is good or bad in art, or of what art is and is not. Instead, works of art become parts of wider philosophical reflections where styles of thought, philosophical problems and works of art interact to transform and broaden the problems. This explains why poststructuralism has had a rich relation to art: in architecture, in literature, in fine art, for example. All the thinkers studied here have developed such fruitful interactions for art and for thought. *The poststructuralist work is often itself part of an aesthetic creative process and a prompt for further creations in art.*

Capitalism and democracy

Poststructuralist works are a radical activity, in the sense of an active process designed to change situations and move them on (but free of fixed norms, values and truths). As such, poststructuralism is political. It changes our world and our views of it across a great range of situations, for example, in terms of our relations to our bodies, in terms of sexuality, gender, relations with others, and in terms of our relations towards the environment or with the unconscious.

This does not mean that poststructuralism is a fixed form of politics in the more restricted sense of government and power within social organizations. One key aspect of poststructuralism is to show that power is not limited to such organizations. This applies both to the limits of government, which extend far beyond laws and political structures, and to the limits of power, where power is to be understood not only as a power over others, but also as a power to change oneself and wider situations from within.

For instance, Foucault traces political power through the historical development of medical practices and institutions, through the shapes of buildings and the technologies of vision and of bio-power (the way power works through biological manipulation of bodies). He also, though, traces the aesthetic power to make and unmake ourselves as subjects and selves. Lyotard describes the power of ideas, such as the image of a possible exhaustion of natural resources and the related dream of a new world. Kristeva describes the revolutionary force of literary works. Deleuze insists on the power of open creativity. Derrida shows the influence of different metaphors, such as the metaphor of light, and their hold on forms of thought.

This extension of the political into a wide range of processes of radical change is one of the great achievements of poststructuralism. It is made possible by the philosophical critique of core forms of knowledge and power, since these are shown to be suffused by much wider and more liberating creative forms that are themselves impossible to identify once and for all.

Poststructuralist politics is an opening up of many different situations and structures on to new possibilities hidden within apparent fixities. This explains the poststructuralist suspicion of the term "possibility" and the preference for the term "virtual". Imagined possibilities are always restrictions based on what we already know, so it is important to define the future in terms of a virtual that does not restrict it through fixed possibilities and probabilities. This is freedom defined as a creative opening on to the unknown, rather than as choice between different options.

Two historical events are emblematic of this way of thinking about the political. The first is the waning of traditional Marxist political movements, in part due to the wider understanding of the failure and repressiveness of Soviet and Maoist regimes in the 1960s, and in part due to the failure of revolutionary movements (for example, in Algeria).

Poststructuralism is post-Marxism and post-Maoism, but it is deeply indebted to Marx. All the poststructuralists treated here have insisted that they continue with the spirit of Marx's work as a movement of the left, as a combat for the margins, for the exploited and the down-trodden. But, equally, all resist the fixed definitions of society, of political structures and of revolutionary movements that come out of Marxism–Leninism or Maoism. *Poststructuralism breaks with Marxism but works within Marx.*

The second emblem is the May 1968 revolutionary movement, with its spontaneity and lack of overarching ideological or organizational unity. May 1968 can be interpreted as showing that a different kind of resistance and revolution is possible: a revolution that works through different structures and bodies, opening them up to new possibilities free of set ideological directions and political logic. *As an heir to 1968, poststructuralism advocates spontaneity, fluidity and openness in political movements of resistance; the revolution of the folding in of limits extends into revolutionary structures and goals.*

Two related general types of criticisms arise out of these relations to Marxism and to May 1968. The first accuses poststructuralism of naivety with respect to political action; it can be made from within liberal political positions or by more traditional Marxists. The second accuses poststructuralism of failing to understand the repressive nature of capitalism and the need to oppose it in terms of alternatives.

The liberal criticism is related to the discussion of Kant and of the Enlightenment set out above. In seeking to highlight the limits and flaws within human rights and within democratic institutions, poststructuralism can be seen as failing to understand that democracy and human rights are the only way to resist evil, ignorance and injustice. Political action should centre on the improvement and extension of democracy guided by a defence of human rights. To deny this is, in the long run, to side naively with evil and repression. However, *it is a mistake to view poststructuralists as opposed to democracy and to human rights.* The opposition is to final accounts of the superiority of specific democratic institutions and human rights. These must be criticized or worked on, not in the hope of overthrowing them, but in the hope of improving our political structures.

The view is that any given democracy and set of rights conceal relations of power and of domination that need to be resisted and criticized.

For poststructuralism, any given democracy and set of rights must be opened on to new possibilities and revitalized, indeed changed radically and riskily. But for poststructuralism this risk for democracy must be taken, as the most open form of government available. It is for a "democracy to come", to use Derrida's expression from his *Politics of Friendship*. There is therefore a refusal to fall into modes of thought that say "either you defend this democracy or democratic decision unconditionally or you are against democracy". Such modes devalue thought and philosophy. Keeping democracy alive through creative transformation is a key part of the politics of poststructuralism.

If there is a critique of this view it comes from a more radical Marxist view that says that this belief in openness fails to take account of the all-encompassing power of capitalism and its relation to failed democracy. On this view, poststructuralists are naive in believing that there is space for resistance from within capitalism and liberal democracy. Instead, there should be a struggle for a post-capitalist economy and post-liberal form of government.

The poststructuralist answer to this double accusation of naivety and resignation is itself twofold. First, poststructuralism does not allow for the utopian form of the argument. There can be no promised state somehow free of all the ills of capitalism. Different economic structures are interlinked and the forms of repression found in each can be found to different degrees in all. *Poststructuralism involves a critique of utopian politics and a reflection on how to retain a drive for a better world without a fixed image of what that world should be.*

Secondly, poststructuralists stress the places in capitalism where it opens up against its most repressive tendencies, such as the invasion and acceleration of time for profit, or the destruction of deep values in the name of comparability. There are places for resistance to these tendencies, in particular, in terms of the creation of new forms of life and relations that are both necessary for capitalism and its thirst for growth and destructive of its worst properties. This is not to be resigned to capitalism; it is to force it to change with a politics of the left, again defined as a politics for ever-changing limits. *Poststructuralism does not promise a pure state, free of current evils; it advocates working for the openings within current states to allow them to change with and for their limits.*

For example, where a cultural or political claim has failed to be recognized as having any value or legitimacy, the point will be to find ways to express its value and legitimacy. Where new forms of poverty, alienation and exploitation emerge, the struggle will be to force structures to open up to new ways of eliminating them. But this is not to dream of a structure where they cannot exist at all. *Poststructuralism is consistent with activism, but not with utopian states.*

The limits of the human

Poststructuralism is a set of experiments on texts, ideas and concepts that show how the limits of knowledge can be crossed and turned into disruptive relations. The range of areas for these applications is very great. It stretches from long historical studies with Foucault, through deconstructions of texts in Derrida, to studies of artworks and linguistics in Kristeva, to studies of structures and sensations in Lyotard, to the creation of new philosophical concepts in Deleuze.

For example, if we take the spaces drawn up by a human being (its body, its consciousness, its mind and ideas, soul and heart), poststructuralist thinkers have broken through each of these spaces to show how any determination of an absolute, pure space cannot hold. The skin is not a firm border between an inside and an outside, but a permeable set of passages that connect the inside to an endless set of causal and wider relations. We are connected to the furthest stars and they are in us.

The birth and death of bodies, or of conscious minds, fails to delimit a pure space of a human life. Both are processes that involve genetic continuity, continuities of ideas and of language, of societies and worlds. This does not mean that there is no such thing as a human life, or that it is not valuable. It means that the life is not an absolute and that its borders are not the greatest certainty on which to construct systems of truths. Human beings do not die, if that is understood as ending finally, once and for all, at a particular point in space and time. They are not born, either, if birth is seen as an absolute point.

Nor is there final certainty when a human mind contains an idea such as "I think". That idea takes its place in an extended and constantly changing tissue of linguistic usage and creativity where "I" and "think" change according to different relations with other words. With them, the idea changes. It has a history and a future that can change it by changing its relation to it. What I think now changes the significance of what I thought then: it was not independent.

Nor is there any final certainty in the limits of human properties, of gender or sex, for example. When we take the presence of a chromosome as the arbiter of a final truth, we miss the extension of that finality, not only in terms of the social, political and ethical meanings of sex and gender, but also as part of a much longer and intertwined series of genetic relations.

The association of the chromosome to the words "male" and "female" already undermines the certainty of its presence through the shifting meanings and significances of the words. The noting of any given fact "here is Y" is already a very wide and complex situation of "Y", of "here" and of "is" in structures of varying differences (of significance, interpretation, feeling). Y is inseparably connected to all things that are different from it; to the point where they are constitutive of Y and where it has no meaningful independent existence. A fact cannot escape its history, its meaning and its future; it does not exist independently of them. This poststructuralist claim extends to personal identity (the self cannot be abstracted from its background) and to the mind (the mind extends to processes way beyond the contents of a particular mind or brain and this extension is both external – outside the mind and body – and internal – deep within the unconscious conditions that determine them).

Perhaps, though, we can claim with structuralism that more secure truths lie in structures rather than individual facts, or the contents of an individual mind, or a particular event. To be human is to have a set of differential relations to other entities: to be an animal in some ways, but not in others, to fit into a set of social relations, inclusions and exclusions, to use language in this or that way. Although changing through time, structures would give us a relative grasp of meaning and truth. We could agree that, at this point, human meant V in relation to X, Y, Z. Poststructuralist thinkers do not deny this kind of truth, but they stress its relativity. How can the statement "at this point" be defined without prejudging the question? The point changes with individual situations and problems. There are events that resist insertion into structures exactly because they force the structures to change.

These events are as important in deciding the significance of the human as apparently settled structures. "Human" is a net thrown over multiple variations and evolutions. The role of thought is to lead and respond to these evolutions, as much as to chart the more fixed states in which they take place. The fixity is always a necessary convention or illusion, rather than a deeper truth. Or perhaps we could claim that the empirical sciences provide a framework of evolving but consistent theories that give us the best available idea of "human". The meaning of "human" must be determined by a set of sciences at a given time, open to revision, but only through well-defined rational scientific methods.

There is no opposition to this view of the importance of empirical sciences from within poststructuralism, except for the value claim "best" and the normative statements "must be" and "only through". Poststructuralist thinkers often rely on the sciences and often model parts of their work on the empirical sciences, but they resist and seek alternatives to the view that science is an ultimate arbiter, or even the final judge of truths.

The limits of science – in terms of what is excluded by it and what is presupposed by any given science – are important factors in working with a concept such as "human". It is not only that literature, art and philosophy, as well as "out-dated" scientific theories, have critical roles to play in terms of the scientific determination of the meaning of "human"; it is that they have a positive constituting role to play. "Human" is always more than what is determined by science. The scientific determination of "human" is always the product of extra-scientific presuppositions.

two

Poststructuralism as deconstruction: Jacques Derrida's *Of Grammatology*

Poststructuralism as deconstruction

Jacques Derrida's *Of Grammatology* [*De la grammatologie*] was first published in French in 1967. It is the most overtly poststructuralist book to be considered here, since its first part deals explicitly and at length with structuralist theories of language through the works of Ferdinand de Saussure and Roman Jakobson, among others. However, in *Of Grammatology*, as elsewhere, deconstruction works within what it follows. The meaning of "post" in poststructuralism is therefore not a final "after" in the sense of a hurdle now passed. Instead, the "post" means "with but also different". Deconstruction is still structuralism, but opened up and transformed.

This transformation takes place through an undermining of structuralism's most fundamental claims to absolute truths, for example, concerning the priority of speech over writing. More widely, *Of Grammatology* develops Derrida's deconstruction of Husserl's phenomenology (begun in Derrida's 1962 introduction to Husserl's *Origin of Geometry*). It also extends the critique of "presence" in phenomenology, and of nature and essence in structuralist theories of language, into the work of Jean-Jacques Rousseau.

Poststructuralism must be thought of as deconstruction, and not the opposite. This is because poststructuralism is nothing other than the series of works that have come to define it. There is no separate determining definition of poststructuralism. This explains why it has been introduced here in terms of a very bare form (the folding of limits back on to knowledge) and of a series of positive and negative properties.

Of Grammatology is one of the key works that define poststructuralism. As such, it allows for a series of relations with other poststructuralist texts such as Lyotard's *Discours, figure* (a book that claims itself as
deconstruction, yet takes some distance from it too). These relations
allow poststructuralism to appear, but it has no existence independent
of them, except as the rather vapid and loose *ism* that emerges more out
of hearsay than close study. However, a first glimpse into the difficulty
and originality of Derrida's book appears with the idea of a selection
of key books and masterworks. A characteristically playful Derridean
chuckle can be heard at the mistake of thinking that we have only the
great book as an expression of the thoughts of the master.

According to its own arguments, *neither the book nor the author exists
as an absolutely independent entity; rather,* Of Grammatology *is a cut-out
from an endless series of texts signed by Derrida and by others.* Derrida is
part of that series and not independent of it. He is there in your hands.
When you write you participate in the series of texts, not by adding
a separate block, but by transforming the endless tissue of texts. This
argument explains why Derrida's work can be very hard to read when
first encountered. If we are used to reading quite short and hermetic
sentences and paragraphs, then his long ones can be hard to follow and
even harder to break down into separate ideas. This is because the very
idea of that kind of separateness is resisted in *Of Grammatology*.

There are at least four quite different general strategies for responding to this difficulty. These allow responses to the frustration of either
looking for key findings and conclusions in vain or trying to keep all
the ideas of a given sentence or paragraph together, only to lose them
through their sheer number and complexity. The strategies are not
mutually exclusive; indeed, they are perhaps best used together. It is
worth noting that the definition of thinking as something strategic, in
the sense of something that responds to and transforms a particular
situation, is an important common feature of poststructuralist works.

According to the first strategy, it is helpful to approach Derrida's work
through the texts he is deconstructing. He is one of the best readers of
other works, in the sense of the most thorough and sensitive. Derrida
is always looking for the greatest source of argumentative strength in
any work, but he is also concerned with important diversions, subtleties
and differences.

There is a French scholarly tradition of an academic exercise called
"*explication de texte*": that is, a very close reading of a text in terms of
its internal coherence, implications, styles and meaning, as well as its
philological and textual roots, connections and contrasts. It is a reading

skill begun very early in French schools and carried through to higher university degrees. The focus is on interpretation, situation and illuminating description, rather than on critique, classification and judgement. The *explication* teaches slow, sensitive, logical and faithful reading. It may have weaknesses in not encouraging quick critical reactions or creative transformations, but that may be compensated by a cautious and attentively respectful care for texts of great power and richness. The stronger the text, the greater the value of an *explication*. A tradition based on quick adversarial critical comment may value knock-down arguments and rapid clear-cut dismissals, but the tradition of the *explication* is geared to drawing the best out of its material, that is, beyond obvious flaws (and their equally obvious rejoinders).

Derrida's books and articles are models of powerful *explications*. His works are more sensitive to variations, better at following logical implications, more adept at capturing different meanings locked in the texts, than most readings of the same initial texts. He writes for a growth in learning, rather than for seekers of quick trenchant truths and judgements. This means that he takes the tradition to another level. It goes beyond an initiation to past greatness, to unlocking its hidden disasters and future potential. His reading is at the same time rigorously true to a given text, but also an often devastating development of unexpected elements. This is because a powerful *explication* must go beyond its text since it is designed to find its weak points, but in relation to its strengths. Derrida's readings reflect on the different arguments in given texts in terms of their hidden presuppositions and extensions; these expand the texts into others and alter the relations meant to hold between their premises and conclusions, and between their theses and demonstrations.

A good approach to *Of Grammatology* is therefore through a short section of the text Derrida is commenting on (Rousseau or Saussure, for example). It is helpful to ask "What is happening?" (to Rousseau, Saussure, Husserl) in a given section of *Of Grammatology*, rather than asking the less subtle and more problematic question of "What is this book about?" *Deconstructions are ongoing processes, rather than fixed findings.*

Avoiding dismissive critique and reductive summary, poststructuralism as deconstruction is a style of writing as a reading of other texts. Derrida always works in a detailed manner within sections taken from other books, essays and articles, hence the very long quoted passages and extensive footnotes in his publications. His readings follow through main arguments and apparently insignificant details and remarks in order to show how they form long dependent chains. These lead to and from the claims to be deconstructed (such as the statement "speech is the origin of writing", for example). At the same time as following these arguments, *Of Grammatology* shows how they are undermined, or shifted, or reversed, in the texts that produce them. For example, Saussure depends on the priority of speech over writing, but he also gives us the resources to deny that priority alongside counter-arguments to it.

Broadly, Derrida shows how Saussure is committed to a heavily determined relation between speech and writing. But Saussure is also committed to the notion of the arbitrariness of the sign. That is, the thing that we perceive (the signifier) and the meaning that we understand (the signified) do not have a necessary relation to one another. A different signifier could be attached to the same signified. The signified does not have to be perceived through a given signifier (any signifier is empty before it becomes part of a sign). This must hold true for the relation of speech to language. Therefore, the relation cannot be determined in the many ways held by Saussure, for example, in terms of privileging a phonetic language.

Therefore, deconstruction is not a form of relativism. It is not that any reading goes. Quite the contrary, the most rigorous reading (as writing) is necessary to find the core interdependencies and most absolute claims and foundations. This rigour, in terms of argument, must be accompanied by a scholarly rigour and a careful inventiveness that finds the minor and excluded parts of a text. These are then shown to be at play within it, shifting the major argument. *As faithful reading, deconstruction is a form of textual positivism.*

In *Of Grammatology*, the major arguments working through texts are described as metaphysics, itself defined as onto-theology. These are complex terms and they will be examined later in this chapter. However, a first sense of their meaning is that scientific, literary and philosophical claims and methods presuppose a given state of the world: a metaphysics.

This metaphysics, according to *Of Grammatology*, has become dominantly onto-theological. That is, the world is thought of in terms of fixed beings and essences defined in terms of identifiable differences. These differences are put into a value system resembling theological distinctions in their, in principle, inviolable assumptions and their categories of good and evil, against and with nature, saved and fallen, of-this-world and of God. These values and differences then guide relations to the future. Acts are thought of as driven towards specific ends defined in terms of the metaphysics. This is the teleological, or goal-driven, aspect of the metaphysics. For example, a theory might have presuppositions about the superiority of Western values. These would imply a metaphysics that distinguished Western reason from others, valuing the former and mistakenly caricaturing the latter. Goals for action would be set according to those Western values, for instance in terms of conversion.

Derrida's work is particularly concerned with these unexamined presuppositions, with their relation to fixed distinctions and with the assumed goodness and naturalness of the goals that follow from them. As such, his work has an important critical role, in the sense of undermining false pretensions to absolute truth. Thus, it is not necessarily the initial supposition that is criticized (for example, reason or a specific scientific assumption). Instead, the metaphysical background is deconstructed. It is revealed and shown to depend on presuppositions that contradict other parts of the theory. It is also shown to be undermined in its claims to pure truths, for example, through its dependence on unexamined metaphors (of light and vision, for instance).

Deconstruction draws out a metaphysical background and its unquestioned role within the power of statements that depend upon it. Therefore, a strong strategy for reading *Of Grammatology* is to follow through a line going from statements to their metaphysical presuppositions. Then, it is to examine how these presuppositions are undermined from within the initial statements. There is often a strongly traditional and logical form to deconstruction: it finds circular arguments and points out contradictions.

In order to follow through these relations between given philosophical and scientific claims and underlying metaphysics, Derrida creates or reinvigorates a series of words that have become keys to understanding deconstruction. These words are important because they have to allow for the critical and transformative work of deconstruction, without themselves giving rise to a new metaphysics. A further useful reading strategy is therefore to try to understand how these words function. This will be done here through the words "presence", "trace", "origin", "play" and "différance" (with an "a"). There are two interesting risks associated with this strategy.

The first risk is to assume that we can arrive at a final definition of these terms. This would contradict the way in which they change in terms of the context they work in. It would also lead to a Derridean metaphysics, if only through a series of negative moves that implied a given order of the world and a specific identity (the trace is neither a form of presence, nor a kind of origin). Such moves themselves presuppose that identity is part of the highest values with respect to truth, as does the search for secure definitions.

The second risk would be to reduce deconstruction to a formula or algorithm. This happened in the early reception of Derrida's work, where he was seen as attempting to reverse key oppositions and hierarchies in the texts to be deconstructed. To deconstruct, would then be, for example, to invert the privileging of voice over writing. This would merely invert the presupposed metaphysics, replacing one by another.

These risks show a particularly difficult problem in the interpretation of Derrida's work. Its resistance to final conclusions and positions makes each point of arrival a temporary one and it makes each definition of deconstruction itself something to be deconstructed. It is then tempting to accuse the philosophy of pointlessness and relativism, since each position seems equally in need of deconstruction and none finally resolves the initial questions and suspicion of metaphysics.

The answer to these critical points is that deconstruction works through what it does: for example, in drawing out and undermining a given relation to metaphysical presuppositions and to onto-theology defined as a theological-like definition of being or existence. It does not have a value through its conclusions, for this would be to set up a new final position. Nor does it work through a sense of direction towards such finality. This would be to commit to another teleology: to the endlessly deferred goals that give the direction. This does not mean that deconstruction falls into a pointless relativism, except if quite extreme views about absolute truths are held. Deconstruction makes a positive stand. For example, *Of Grammatology* attempts to undo ethnocentrism and anthropocentrism: the privileging of a given ethnicity (usually Western) and the privileging of a particular conception of man over other forms of existence.

Deconstruction works to release writing from the grip of an inner voice and from speech. It shows the metaphysical presuppositions of structuralist metaphysics. None of this work is final or arrives at final positions. Nonetheless, there is change and, relatively, a change for the better. A further critical remark comes in at this point. Can there really be change for the better and a value in Derrida's work if deconstruction destroys, or undermines, or breeds ignorance of higher values? In particular, is it the case that deconstruction works against the empirical sciences and their resistance to falsehood and to ignorance?

The straightforward answer to these criticisms is that there is a long consideration of science in *Of Grammatology*. This consideration explains a closeness to, but also a critical distance from science. It will be covered in a later section. Deconstruction is never simply anti-science. Rather, it investigates the relation of metaphysics and onto-theology to science. This, in itself, could be a flaw. For example, what of the claim that modern empirical science is free of metaphysical presuppositions, or so aware of them that it has inbuilt protection against them through scientific methodology? Could it be that we can escape what Derrida calls onto-theology, but that *Of Grammatology* brings us back to it through the hope of undermining or transforming it? Is Derrida committed to the claim that metaphysics is inescapable? In which case, is he committed to a position that contradicts itself (since what could be the foundation for such a claim in deconstruction)?

Such questions provide a fourth strategy for reading *Of Grammatology*. Many of the patterns of arguments that run through the book are explicit or implicit responses to these critical questions. That deconstruction and poststructuralism are deeply self-critical has often been overlooked. This explains their at times overly rarefied quality, as if too many possible criticisms and self-criticisms have been taken on board, leaving no substance.

It is therefore useful to work through *Of Grammatology* in response to a specific question. Here, the question will be: what is the relation of deconstruction's work on metaphysics to its work on science? For the fullest interpretation of the book, such questions and strategies should not be taken alone. As a complex work of philosophy, it allows for a fruitful combination of critical scrutiny, close analysis of its key terms, study through the wider texts and tracing of its key claims on metaphysics and onto-theology.

Keywords of deconstruction

To understand some of the keywords in *Of Grammatology* it is best to ask not what they mean, but what they do. The words do not stand for things that can be easily captured and identified; rather, they explain processes at work in texts. These processes are to be deconstructed, but they are also part of the deconstruction. So Derrida's readings seek out and exploit the strength of the arguments to be deconstructed. He does not focus on the weaknesses of a position or tradition, but shows how its strengths work against themselves at their highest and most crucial points. Poststructuralism as deconstruction is not concerned with the effects of a position, but with the relation between its foundations and its most distant claims.

Here are some keywords and processes from *Of Grammatology*: origin, presence, trace, différance and play.

Origin

The arguments and claims that run through a given text can often be traced back to a claim about an origin. This is a first and most pure point from whence everything else descends. This descent is seen as a fall, that is, as a loss of purity and value, but it is also a source, the only way to explain and justify what remains of value. Origins therefore also work as goals. We search to recapture what we have lost and, hence, where we came from also becomes where we should still go. Origins are the grounds for feelings such as nostalgia and for negative processes such as unfavourable judgements on everything that follows the origin but fails to shine like it.

When we read closely, however, following Derrida's deconstructions, we find that there are no pure origins or first points. Origins are always projections from what is supposed to follow from them. The origin is always infected by what follows it. *Origins are therefore also themselves originated: the origin has an origin.* The origin must itself be manufactured and is part of an endless chain, rather than a first beginning.

Presence

In the struggle with scepticism – with the many doubts and uncertainties that can be deployed against knowledge – texts lead to points that cannot be doubted or ought not to be dubitable. These can be named as points of presence, where there is no mediation between the phenomenon and the thought (and hence no space for doubt). In presence, the phenomenon is the thought.

Presence is the point where a text finds its most pure truth. But deconstructions show this purity to be illusory. External mediations can be found within presence. These bring complexity into presence. What appeared to be unmediated intuitions are seen to contain contradictory levels and parts. These allow for the return of multiple interpretations, of reasons to doubt and of opportunities to disagree. With this return there is also an opening up of presence.

Each deconstruction of presence shows it to be an illusion: a cover over much more complex and intertwined relations. The unmediated point is mediated and constructed, and hence open to deconstruction. *Presence is part of an economy of truth, that is, its power is dependent on many claims that lie outside it and that circulate within it*, for example, claims about origins. When we think that we have found presence, in the intuition "I think", in another's promise such as "I do", or in the second inner voice we can turn to when writing, we still depend on a language that unfolds with its own patterns and mediations, with its extended doubts and equivocations.

Trace

The origin and the point of presence have to be signified in texts; something has to stand for them or represent them. There have to be signs for them. But signs in language contain the trace of their contexts, of their histories and of their futures. So any sign, any event, is marked by things that lie outside it. It is not an unalloyed presence, but the trace of the processes that came to make it. Instead of well-determined independent signs, Derrida follows multiple processes through traces in the text.

These processes of tracing do not have internal limits, in the form of a necessary logic or grammar, so there is no fixed truth or presence in the form of the trace. Nor do they have external limits, in the sense of something independent of traces (the voice, inner sense, flesh, matter, metaphysical substance). We can find traces there too. *There is nothing outside the text as tracing.*

But do traces not have to be perceived? If they have to be perceived, is it not as something identifiable as "this trace"? If this is the case, then are structuralists not right to study structures of differences between traces and their relation to meanings? Are empirical scientists not right to seek out identifiable results to well-defined experiments?

In *Of Grammatology*, Derrida shows how even the perception of a trace is not a point of presence. Traces only appear on condition of appearing with their tracks and complex relations, rather than free of them. So perception picks up on a tracing, rather than a well-defined trace. The definition only appears afterwards when the perception is falsely abstracted from its background.

Différance

The term différance gives a further account of the trace against demands for identity (it is treated at length in Derrida's essay "Différance" in *Margins of Philosophy*). Différance is a structure of identifiable differences – that any trace depends on – but it is also a process of differing that cannot be reduced to chains of identities. Rather, it is the reason why such chains are always open and incomplete.

This openness and incompleteness are not to be defined in terms of an open set of possible interpretations, or in terms of a series that can always be added to. *Instead, différance is the condition for the openness and incompleteness of any identifiable part of the chain.* It is not that there is something rendered open by interpretations. It is not that there is an identifiable series rendered uncertain by the possibility of new elements.

Différance is a condition for the relation of trace to text: any trace only appears because it can differ and because it differs in all its relations. So when you write your name, or do something as simple as ticking a box, that name and box do not have an existence independent of their differing relations to other traces: not as relations between fixed entities that can be added to or commented on, but as fluid relations between fluid entities. It is never just a cross or a tick.

Furthermore, différance cannot be set at a particular time; rather, it is a series of differing relations through time, where time cannot be thought of as external to those relations. Neither can différance be set within a particular set of texts or media. Wherever there are traces, there is différance. Its differing cannot be restricted in principle for any given trace or relation between a trace and a fixed meaning. Derrida shows how meaning and tracing run away and constantly change with no pre-set limits of appropriateness or property.

Play

If différance still seems to indicate a process outside structures, the term "play" is used by Derrida to show how structures have a looseness and openness at their very heart. In the same way as a mechanism can have some looseness or play in it, he shows how different structures are open to varieties of interpretations and deductions. These show that there is no single meaning, or single line of argument, but many different ones that open up where there is play in the system.

In addition to bringing differing processes closer to structure, the term "play" also counters the view that *Of Grammatology* is a work of negative criticism. It is not that different argumentative possibilities and interpretations merely show the falsehood or imprecision of a unique position or claim to presence. Rather, play must be taken in an affirmative sense of play: in the context of joyful gaming, where opening up is not for negative purposes, but for the positive value of new desires and fields to expand into.

This sense of affirmation is very important. It shows how the different terms used by Derrida complement each other, despite appearing to have very close meanings or, more properly, functions. The terms are close, but they cannot be reduced to one another. There is a deliberate sense of play even in Derrida's own terms. Each opens up in different ways and allows for variations on themes. *Deconstruction is affirmative in allowing for play, openness and creativity at its heart, right into its most powerful terms.*

Perhaps this goes some way to explaining the richness and quantity of Derrida's output. He is constantly varying, refining and adding to his own work. To use another term from *Of Grammatology*, there is always already a "supplement" within any given text, a point where play can begin. Deconstruction must therefore not only be understood in the sense of demolition, but in the sense of constructing otherwise in order to deconstruct.

Since there is such an insistence on process and practice in poststructuralism as deconstruction, it is important to move on from this external account of Derrida's terms into a reading of his text. The final chapter of *Of Grammatology* puts all these terms into practice in a deconstruction of Rousseau's account of a fall from presence. For Rousseau, the sentimental presence of an unarticulated sentiment (a scream, for instance) falls into and is lost in articulated writing. Writing betrays and loses sentiment.

Rousseau judges this fall as both necessary and negative. The fall is something we have to work with, but also work against. Derrida deconstructs these value judgements, for example, in the following passage:

> Such is the situation of writing within the history of metaphysics: a debased, lateralized, repressed, displaced theme, yet exercising a permanent and obsessive pressure from the place where it remains held in check. A feared writing must be cancelled because it erases the presence of the self-same [*propre*] within speech. (OG: 270)

In this last chapter, "From/Of the Supplement to the Source", Derrida is showing how the source, or origin, has a supplement already held within it: writing as supplement to pure sentiment. There is no origin without that supplement, but neither is there a supplement without an origin (hence his play on the twin senses of the French preposition "*du*" as "of" and "from", which required the slightly awkward title in translation).

In that chapter, Derrida reads Rousseau's text to find the play at the origin of language. He finds it in Rousseau's admittance of a natural and necessary fall from sentiment into language. He also finds it where language as speech already has the characteristics of writing, because an original scream has to be separated into different sounds and hence into parts for more complex communication.

When examined closely, even the original scream, the point of presence where there should be no writing, is already a trace; it is inscribed and has a complex structure. Rather than being purely present, it is caught in a differing movement, back through its different variations and reactions, and through the different ways it has taken position in writing (and will continue to take place in writing). Derrida searches for the signs of a supplement to an origin in Rousseau's arguments, despite the fact that these are designed to show that there are none. Rousseau's obsessive pursuit of writing is already one of these signs (of sentiment implicated in writing).

In *Of Grammatology*, Derrida also uncovers a role for writing within what seems to be only proper to speech. Thus, even in feelings such as fear and pleasure, he finds writing at work even within Rousseau's accounts. In Rousseau (and Condillac's) work, fear and pleasure are not only moments of presence, they are also moments of delay and mediation. For example, fear is communicated and expressed in a metaphorical form where the expression of fear indicates what is feared (when the size of the threat is indicated in a gesture, for instance).

In Rousseau's work, as read by Derrida, pleasure is not only the apparently full pleasure taken in something, but also a relation to desire and hence to the representation of the thing. If this pleasure in relation to a thing can be both immediate and mediated, it is because there is no pure presence in pleasure: it is always already related to desire and hence to writing. "What dislocates presence introduces différance and delay, spacing between desire and pleasure. Articulated language, knowledge and work, the anxious research of learning, are nothing but the spacings between two pleasures" (OG: 280).

Rousseau's text is therefore the start of its own deconstruction: "Was not the great project of the *Confessions* also to 'enjoy ... once more when I desire it'?" (OG: 280). This repetition of the "once more" is one of Derrida's ways into differing, since that repetition depends on traces and on writing. It introduces a gap into pleasure. This gap is widened where it is thought of in terms of desire. This is because desire, according to Rousseau, depends on an absence of pleasure, but also on a representation of its possibility (I desire X, although X is not there in some way).

All the main characteristics of deconstruction are at work in *Of Grammatology*'s last chapter. There is the close reading of other texts, the extension of texts across Rousseau's works and into others (Condillac and Derrida). There is the undermining of presence and of the origin, through supplements in their supposedly undivided hearts. There is the critique of the metaphysics dependent on presence and origins: in this case, the metaphysics of the priority of feelings over writing.

It could be objected that none of this work supports the view of the radical openness of the trace and of différance. All Derrida has shown is a practical opening in a particular case. This is to miss two important points. First, Derrida is working on foundational and paradigmatic cases that are signs of a much wider metaphysics. It is not so much that he is saying that the same can definitely be done elsewhere; rather, he is seeking to lead into such work and to undermine arguments for its impossibility.

Secondly, many of the connections, concepts and arguments drawn through Rousseau can be found in other texts. So there is never a deconstruction of a single text, author and argument. Instead, there is the start of an ongoing process of deconstruction that implicates many texts to different degrees and across different distances. In that sense there is a radical openness, for instance, through the double structure of nature as pure origin, but also in the sense of natural fall or decline.

On the other hand, it could be objected again that all of this is purely negative. It is a form of critique dependent on prior constructions, lacking their positive creativity and contradicting the supposedly affirmative sense of Derrida's term "play". He could be accused of living off genuinely constructive thinkers, such as Rousseau, while bringing none of his benefits in political thinking and social reform.

This objection is countered further on in *Of Grammatology*, where Derrida uses the term "play" to respond to the idea of the negativity of deconstruction. It is not the case that openness to change can only bring negative effects; instead, looseness and play within systems can be ethically positive. The chance involved in the change from one structure to another, which always appears bad from within a known structure, need not be so: "This chance may be thought, as it is here the case, negatively as catastrophe, or affirmatively as play" (OG: 294). In order to see the full force of this argument it is important to return to Derrida's work on metaphysics.

Deconstruction and metaphysics

In the work on Rousseau, Derrida draws a complicated connection between metaphysics and violence. This link is also drawn in, for example, "Violence and Metaphysics", his important essay on Emmanuel Levinas, in *Writing and Difference* (a collection that appeared at the same time as *Of Grammatology*). This connection with violence explains Derrida's focus on metaphysics. He is concerned with the violent inclusions and exclusions, omissions and valuations implicit in metaphysical distinctions and hierarchies, as well as metaphysical processes.

This connection is, however, a double-edged and perplexing one. This is because attacks on metaphysics as grounds for violence, for example, in terms of a distinction between rational animals (human beings) and mere animals, can themselves lead to further violent metaphysical distinctions (all sentient animals versus plants, for instance).

This is the pattern that Derrida uncovers in his reading of Rousseau and the structuralist Lévi-Strauss in the chapter in *Of Grammatology* called "The Violence of the Letter: From Lévi-Strauss to Rousseau". Both authors see the fall from sentiment and from the voice into writing as a source of violence, avoidable by a return to the presence of the sentiment or feeling (of fear or pleasure, for example). But Derrida's counter is that this gives rise to a new metaphysical violence and exclusion. The communal aspects of sentiment and presence presupposed by the voice do violence to the radical otherness of other beings. That is, by assuming that this presence is the same for all, others are given an identity that we should not give them.

The assumption that there is presence in the voice, together with the accusation that all metaphysics as violence begins with writing, is itself a form of violence done to writing and to speech. Even in answering the question of violence and metaphysics, there can be no return to presence but, instead, there should be a writing of radical différance and otherness: "The ethics of speech is the *delusion* of presence mastered" (OG: 139).

This delusion or lure, both trap and enticing falsehood, leads to the attraction of a morality based on presence and to the denial of the ethical value of writing. In response, Derrida insists on the ethical value of the deferral of presence and on the way it allows for a very different "presence": the presence of the other. There is a presence of the other as something that cannot be present:

> To recognise writing in speech, that is to say différance and the absence of speech, is to begin to think the lure. There is no ethics without the presence *of the other* but also, and consequently, without absence, dissimulation, detour, différance, writing.   (OG: 140)

The distinction drawn between morality and ethics lies in the constant deferral of ethics, in the sense of never defining or fixing the other. This is an important aspect of poststructuralism. It turns away from structuralist method and its metaphysical presuppositions, because they presuppose that the other can be defined and because the other is defined on the grounds of a particular morality.

For Derrida, this morality must be particular – for example, of the West – because the points where it rests on a supposed universal, that is, on presence, turn out to be more complex and divisible; they are chance-driven grounds rather than universal foundations. Where morality hopes to be founded on the certainty of presence, deconstruction only finds the differing of traces and the movement of différance.

Early sections in *Of Grammatology* explore these metaphysical forms of violence. For example, in discussing "the inside and the outside" Derrida notes how Saussure's structuralist linguistics depends on limits drawn between forms of being (speech, language, body, writing). These limits presuppose inclusions and exclusions, with well-determined valuations (inside better/outside worse, for instance). But such valuations are illegitimate when viewed as anything other than contingent and particular. The structuralist claims to be making general claims; but these are, in fact, particular. Thereby, violence is done to other excluded particulars and to the very possibility of cases that defy the original metaphysical presuppositions. In a sense, it is like saying to someone that they cannot be what they are, because no such category is possible ("It is. Here I am").

A series of important critical questions and difficult problems must be raised at this point:

- How can deconstruction avoid setting up a secure ground of its own, if it is to argue against other metaphysical positions?
- Do Derrida's main terms of "traces" and "différance", commit him to a metaphysics, in particular, if they are accompanied by absolute claims, such as "endless" deferral, "ungraspable" trace and "absolute" or "infinite" otherness? He is always careful to avoid these terms, but are they not implied?
- Even if we accept that there is some kind of violence implicated in any metaphysics, is this not a relative violence, where some metaphysics can claim to be less violent than others? If this is the case, why would it really be less violent to try to deconstruct all metaphysics, rather than find the "least bad" one?
- Should moral action not be based on exactly the kind of metaphysics that Derrida deconstructs, that is, one that allows for clear

definitions and secure judgements, rather than much vaguer post-
ponements?

To answer these questions it is helpful to turn to the section "The Hinge"
in the first part of *Of Grammatology*, where Derrida develops a response
to structuralism and to metaphysics that applies specifically to his own
work.

A little earlier in the book, in a section on being, he raises the problems of metaphysics in a historical context, notably, through Heidegger's
reading of Nietzsche as the last metaphysician. Derrida draws an important lesson from the indecision of both thinkers on the question of
the relation of philosophy to metaphysics. He claims that this indecision, leading to a trembling on the border between metaphysics and its
destruction, was "proper" to the passage between a metaphysical (Hege-
lian) epoch and an epoch of deconstruction. The latter epoch cannot
simply be "post" or "new". It has to work within what it follows:

> The movements of deconstruction do not destroy structures from
> the outside. They are not possible and effective, nor can they take
> accurate aim, except by inhabiting those structures. Inhabiting
> them *in a certain way*, because one always inhabits, and all the
> more when one does not suspect it. Operating necessarily from
> the inside, borrowing all the strategic and economic resources of
> subversion from the old structure, borrowing them structurally,
> that is to say without being able to isolate their elements and
> atoms, the enterprise of deconstruction always in a certain way
> falls prey to its own work. (OG: 24)

This passage gives us some answers to the questions raised above. It
is never a matter of going beyond metaphysics, but one of working to
loosen it from within. As such, deconstruction does not have its own
ground; instead, it has a series of strategic ways of drawing out and
subverting claims to truth in other structures. It is a matter not of defining independent entities, but of making connections that undermine
prioritized ones and open up minor or discarded ones.

Furthermore, deconstruction does not set itself up as independent
from what it deconstructs, even in the sense of escaping its problems
or flaws. These will recur in the work of deconstruction and, therefore,
it needs to deconstruct itself. This deconstruction of deconstruction is
an open process or task, rather than a task guided by any given values
or aimed at any identifiable term.

So, in terms of the inclusions and exclusions described above, deconstruction does not aim to move to a world where there are no inclusions and exclusions. Nor does it seek to show that certain inclusions and exclusions are necessarily illegitimate. Instead, it seeks to show how systems based on them contain the seeds of their own contradiction and destruction, hence the title of the section "The Outside is the Inside". When we encounter such fundamental distinctions we find that they are based on traces that cross the distinction: the inside is the outside.

A shallow criticism of Derrida's statement that there is no outside of the text can be dismissed at this point. He can be attacked for implying that things that are patently not textual (objects, ideas, feelings) are in fact nothing but words. But this is not his point at all. Rather, his deconstruction of clear distinctions between the inside and the outside of fields shows that the boundary between text and what lies outside it cannot be finally set or claimed to be impermeable. We find writing at work in things that are claimed to be outside it or independent of it.

This does not mean that the distinction can simply be erased and forgotten, or moved beyond. Rather, Derrida's point is that it is not absolute and that we must think within the breakdown of the distinction. This is why he crosses out the "is" in the title to the section, using Heidegger's notation for Being. When we say that something is something else we conflate the two in a single well-determined essence. Derrida wants to resist this identification of two terms joined by a claim about being (X is Y): "Now we must think that writing is at the same time more exterior to speech, not being its 'image' or 'symbol', and more interior to speech, which is itself already a writing" (OG: 46).

It is now possible to understand a further response by Derrida to the questions asked above. The questions are in some sense illegitimate. They are the wrong kind of question, because they ask for well-determined yes/no, inside/outside, for/against styles of answer. His work shows that this kind of distinction misses the way in which things are implicated in one another:

> Here, as elsewhere, to pose the problem in terms of choice, to oblige or to believe oneself obliged to answer it by a yes or no, to conceive of appurtenance as an allegiance or non-appurtenance as plain speaking, is to confuse very different levels, paths and styles. In the deconstruction of the archē, one does not make a choice. (OG: 62)

This "archē" can be thought of as an original condition, for example of writing, such as a deep grammar, or of speech, such as a basic general phonetics shared by all tongues. Derrida's point is that we have to think in terms of the relation between the condition and the conditioned as a mutual implication and ongoing transformation – a deconstruction – and not as a choice between either general conditions or chaos and confusion.

This refusal of questions that demand either/or answers is a sign of the radical nature of poststructuralism as deconstruction. It does not take its place in a set of pre-established intuitions about the nature of the world: about space, time and existence. Instead, in *Of Grammatology* Derrida shows how traditional concepts of time cannot account for the structure of the trace: "The concepts of present, past, and future, everything in the concepts of time and history that assumes their classical evidence – the general metaphysical concept of time – cannot describe the structure of the trace adequately" (OG: 67, translation modified).

These concepts are inadequate because they presuppose forms of presence that contradict the absence of clear limits for the trace. For example, any trace in the present is connected to the past and to the future in a way that denies their independence and their succession. The past is with the present and with the future in such a way as to deny that it is past in some final way and therefore absent from the present and the future.

In turn, Derrida extends these remarks on time to similar problems concerning the role of death in metaphysics. If death is associated with finitude, that is, with the necessary end of an individual ground for existence – a thinking consciousness or human being, for example – then the trace and the endless structure of différance run counter to it.

Consciousness cannot be said to be above all consciousness of its own finitude, but neither can any moment of consciousness be said to be free of death as an undermining of its presence. This is because, as presence, consciousness is always undermined through the web of traces that extend beyond any given boundary: traces of the death and destruction of identities. But, exactly because it is extended in this way, consciousness is then not defined essentially by its finitude: death is a form of transforming continuity, rather than a simple end (or the continuity of part of an identity).

The metaphysics of death, of consciousness and of subjectivity must therefore be re-examined with deconstruction and thought otherwise. The following passage brings these themes together in the context of a "becoming absent" implied by the spacing of writing, that is, that any well-defined space is extended, stretched and rendered multiple by the way it is written (has been written and will be written):

> Spacing as writing is the becoming-absent and the becoming-unconscious of the subject. By the movement of its drift/derivation [*dérive*] the emancipation of the sign constitutes in return the desire of presence. That becoming – or that drift/derivation – does not befall the subject which would choose it or would passively let itself be drawn along by it. As the subject's relationship with its own death, this becoming is the constitution of subjectivity. (OG: 69)

Derrida reverses and extends traditional senses of the relation of the subject to death. Death in deconstruction is the property of all signs as things that become absent. But it only has this sense because of a counter-desire for presence. Presence and becoming absent are conditions for one another in a way that belies any sense of the independence of presence.

In turn, this counters the definition of death as the death of subjects above all. On a different level it also counters the claim that deconstruction somehow leaves presence behind. It does not; rather, it adds to it and thereby changes its status. Subjectivity and the definition of death in terms of subjectivity are constituted by processes that are themselves conditions for writing and texts.

In *Of Grammatology*, these processes are described in terms of the "hinge". Any trace, any perceived sign is the coming together of a disappearing presence (everything we believe to have grasped and hold beyond doubt) with an endless series of multiple meanings: "The hinge marks the impossibility that a sign, the unity of a signifier and a signified, be produced within the plenitude of a present and an absolute presence" (OG: 69). Two remarks follow from this claim to impossibility. First, it shows how far deconstruction and poststructuralism rest on deeply philosophical forms of thought. They are always more than methods in the arts, humanities and social sciences. They are creative but also sceptical claims about fundamental ways of thinking about existence and the world.

Poststructuralism as deconstruction is a new way of thinking with the metaphysical history, desires and violence of thought (to use "about" rather than "with" here would give a false sense of standing apart from metaphysics and of being able to judge it). Deconstruction is a critical and creative engagement with what we believe to be possible, necessary, true, fully sensed, understood and absolute.

Secondly, this focus on metaphysics sets Derrida in an uneasy relation to science, in terms of either claims to be free of metaphysical presuppositions through its empirical and falsifiable basis or as providing evidence for forms of truths that counter the deconstruction of forms of presence. This unease is commented on with a great acuity in this passage from the hinge section from *Of Grammatology*:

> It is precisely these concepts that permitted the exclusion of writing: image or representation, sensible and intelligible, nature and culture, nature and technics, etc. They are solidary with all metaphysical conceptuality and particularly with a naturalist, objectivist, and derivative determination of difference between outside and inside. (OG: 71)

Given Derrida's work to show the play of writing within structures that appear to exclude it, such as the voice, it seems that it must also be set against concepts that are a set to work in science such as nature, culture, representation and technique.

In scientific practice and theory, we find notions of theoretical representation, of data (in the sense of sensible data, which can then become intelligible), of the explanatory power of images, of nature, of objectivity and of distinctions between what has to be counted as within a given field and independent of it. If science rests on these concepts, it seems that it must be viewed in opposition to deconstruction. But if deconstruction must deny both science and these concepts, then is it in the difficult position of having to repudiate science?

Deconstruction and science

Can Derrida's work provide answers to the following questions:

- Should we not move beyond metaphysics and its deconstruction into a properly scientific age grounded in the empirical sciences and their methodologies?
- Does contemporary science not provide us with the kind of secure truths (and ways of testing and discarding them) that deconstruction denies through its dependence on the study of conditions of writing?

The chapter "Of Grammatology as a Positive Science" in *Of Grammatology* is a direct response to these questions. The details of the title already answer certain basic objections and misunderstandings. It is not the case that Derrida ignores science; he is concerned with questions about the relation between science and deconstruction. The chapter also provides a more precise sense of that concern. Derrida reflects on a relation to positive science. This means that he is directly addressing questions of the role of empirical evidence in grammatology and deconstruction. That is, do they have positive evidence as bases for either their verification or their falsification? Are there experiments and definitions of kinds of data that allow their theories to be verified or shown to be false?

There are strong parallels between this concern with science and the psychoanalyst Jacques Lacan's later work, in particular, in its relation to mathematics. The question "Does psychoanalysis have a scientific basis?" raises the same kinds of issues as the question "What is the relation of deconstruction to science?" This parallel is all the more interesting because the deconstruction of the subject outlined above intersects with Lacan's work on the ego and on the unconscious in his development of Freudian psychoanalysis. The connections between poststructuralism and Lacan are considered at greater length here in Chapter 6, on Kristeva. It is important to note at this point that there are strong connections, but also very great critical contrasts between deconstruction and Lacan's work.

Straight after the title of his chapter, Derrida shows why such questions are important and very difficult to answer. A key aspect of deconstruction is to search for the conditions for its own enquiry and for other sciences. This search is different from positive sciences. His claim is that it is prior to them: "Graphematics or grammatography ought no longer to be presented as sciences; their goal should be exorbitant when compared to grammatological knowledge" (OG: 74). So it is not that Derrida denies the possibility of knowledge on a positive evidential and consistent logical basis. Rather, it is that he considers thinking about writing as deconstruction as somehow impossible to do on the model of the positive sciences. The reason for this is that, when we look for positive bases, we find none. For example, the signs that make up writing, its historical origins, or its basic structures (logical or structural) are always dissolved into further processes.

Simple accounts of why positive evidence is problematic for Derrida can be summed up from earlier sections here: the origin is never a final origin; the presence of either signifier (what is perceived) or signified (the meaning) is replaced by the movement of the trace in différance. In other words, wherever we search for a clearly identified thing that can stand as the basic evidential ground, we find that it itself rests on further endless processes that dissolve its identity as ground.

Such accounts, though, do not do enough to address the initial questions about science, since these are not so much about why deconstruction cannot be a straightforward positive science, but about the consequences of this impossibility and about whether it is a correct position to take. It is therefore important to add the following points from the discussion of science in *Of Grammatology*:

- Derrida's approach to questions of science is through a deconstruction of historical attempts to ground a science of writing.
- This history is one of mistaken claims to grounds, where in fact there are further presuppositions that deny that claim.
- These historical contradictions and processes raise questions about whether any science of writing is possible.
- They also raise questions of how we should approach questions of a science of writing.
- Derrida suggests that writing is resistant to being thought of in terms of positive science.
- This leads him to distinguish thought and science, where thought does not deny science, but lays claim to extend beyond it and to have a deconstructive relation to its declarations of priority and greater truthfulness.

The final passage of the chapter on science is telling in terms of these points, since it sums them up by drawing the crucial distinction between thought and science, but without denying the possibility of either one:

> The constitution of a science or a philosophy of writing is a necessary and difficult task. But a thought of the trace, of différance or of reserve, having arrived at these limits [of science and philosophy] and repeating them ceaselessly, must also point beyond the field of the *epistémè* [of philosophy of knowledge].
> (OG: 93)

By limits of science, Derrida means historical limits in terms of theoretical, practical, economic and social presuppositions. Science does not take place in a vacuum. Wherever there is a claim to positive evidence, or to objective methods, or to a settled neutral theory, series of inclusions and exclusions, presuppositions regarding presence and origins define limits for that claim. It is the role for thought as deconstruction to think beyond those limits.

So deconstruction must interact with science and depends upon it. It is not opposed to science. Instead, it has a different relation to the limits of science than science itself. It opens on to those limits in a different way to science. This is not the same openness that we find in the logic of scientific discovery in terms of openness to new theories and falsification of current ones. Derrida is considering thought as an openness to deconstructions of our most firmly held metaphysical positions, including those of science.

This raises an important question in terms of whether science is free of metaphysical presuppositions, or can be free of them. This question sheds further light on what *Of Grammatology* is doing in terms of science. It is an attempt to show that, historically, scientific approaches to writing have failed to escape metaphysical presuppositions. That failure is also a failure to escape ethical and political inclusions, exclusions and forms of power: "the solidarity among ideological, religious, scientific-technical systems, and the systems of writing which were therefore more and other than 'means of communication' or vehicles of the signified, remains indestructible" (OG: 93).

Again, a lot hinges on the apparent contradiction between a historical argument that must be contingent and open to revision and a claim to indestructibility. The stronger version of objections to Derrida could be that certain advances in the philosophy and practice of science have led to positions that are not open to the kind of deconstruction practised on historical cases.

A possible answer to this objection is that Derrida's work in *Of Grammatology* is not narrowly historical and hence contingent. The deconstruction of sciences of writing leads to a way of thinking about writing that makes a strong case for thinking that there is promise in any deconstruction of a claim to a science free of metaphysical presuppositions. However, this can only ever be promise and not certainty. Deconstruction depends on future practical performances, rather than settled truths that lie outside history and practice.

Clarity, ethics and politics

When Derrida died in 2004, highly charged debates about the value of his work erupted again, even in the obituary pages. Is his work deliberately and dishonestly obscure? Or is it one of the most important currents in twentieth-century thought? The tone of such debates is often unseemly, none more so than in the weeks following his death.

The level of ignorance can also be quite shocking, in so far as some critics attack him on a very sketchy knowledge of his books and on the disgraceful premises of hearsay, arguments from authority ("well X says so") or instant dismissal for being too "difficult". Two related issues can help to give more direction to the debate. First, it is generated by views about an ethics of reading, that is, about what duty we owe to a text in terms of its interpretation (for example, in terms of whether a reading should always be literal, or in terms of how much effort we should put into understanding difficult or foreign texts, in the sense of involving strange ideas or of using unfamiliar idioms). Secondly, it is driven by views on the political and philosophical importance of clarity and accessibility, that is, about the political value of clear exposition and position-taking and the philosophical value of avoidance of obscurities, confusion and contradiction. These views connect the values of an open society with values about clear and consistent communication. It is the connection that matters here rather than the society. The value of openness is shared by both sides of the debate, but the form taken by openness and the relation of that form to clarity is not.

It is important to note that the first issue matters whether Derrida is well known and influential or not. We can owe a duty of careful reading to even the least well-known text, for example, when we struggle to interpret an apparently irrational scribble handed to us in desperation by a passer-by. The second issue, on the other hand, grows in importance with the influence of Derrida's work. At its most vociferous it leads into quite violent demands to unmask dangerous charlatans.

In terms of an ethics of reading, *Of Grammatology* shows that Derrida has reasons for writing in the way he does. Irrespective of whether we finally agree or disagree with them, we cannot be discharged of a duty to try to understand his work prior to dismissing it. He is not deliberately trying to fool anyone. On this count at least his critics have no grounds for attacking him.

The following remark was made by the philosopher Brian Leiter soon after Derrida's death:

> But he [Derrida] devoted his professional life to obfuscation and increasing the amount of ignorance in the world: by "teaching" legions of earnest individuals how to read badly and think carelessly. He may have been a morally decent man, but he led a bad life, and his legacy is one of shame for the humanities.
>
> (Leiter Reports, 31 October 2004)

But Derrida did not "devote" his life to ignorance, bad thinking and carelessness. He tried to think through a series of difficult questions in as clear a way as he thought possible, given the series of philosophical problems he was dealing with. Derrida reads other writers closely, with care, and with erudition. His work tries to open texts to wider connections, but also to submit them to rigorous scrutiny as to their presuppositions. He teaches us to have an eye for details and an ear for style and for the complex layers of a text (its manifold meanings that allow for irony, for example).

It is cause for melancholy to see Leiter making moral judgements about good and bad lives with so little regard for grief and for the values of restraint, reflection and respect in the period after a person's death. But that melancholy has little place in Derrida's work. It is more productive to observe that ignorance of the depth and precision of Derrida's readings reflects the narrow definition of thought that he deconstructed over a long series of precise and well-researched arguments. It also shows the contradictions that this narrowness leads into, for example, in the intellectually sloppy claim about Derrida's own supposed carelessness.

Equally, the claim that Derrida's works misled others shows exactly the kind of exclusive and insensitive judgements of others that Derrida sought to reveal in metaphysics and to avoid in his own writing. Leiter's statements about decency and moral goodness in a life and in a man show an unsubtle and thoughtless tendency to generalization, both in terms of the possibility of associating a life or a being with a single property or quality and in terms of thinking that lives and works can be judged in abstraction.

Yet, Leiter and Derrida's other superficial critics have a different and stronger argument to fall back on. Derrida's difficult style can be accused of being politically dangerous because it undermines the role of clear and open debate and reflection in open societies. Philosophy can be seen as the guardian of such debates. It then arbitrates over valid and invalid arguments and draws out their presuppositions and premises. Philosophy can help us to reflect on the good and the true in an accessible and clear manner. There is great value to this kind of openness, for example, through investigative journalism that unmasks lies and hypocrisies, or through the demonstration of contradictions or of troubling premises in the arguments of politicians and policy-makers.

The main question is not so much about these values, however, as about the directness of the relation between philosophy and society. Is philosophy the direct and present source of such values in society? Does philosophy prepare for these values and over what time frame? Or does it uphold them in the present? Is the role of philosophy to continue to criticize such values, even when they seem to be widely accepted, since these values themselves emerged over a long period of time through such criticism?

Is there something more to philosophy than upholding clarity and openness, if so what is it and can it be pursued under the stricture that thought must be clear and accessible? Indeed, is the clarity advocated by Derrida's critics really clear, in the sense of allowing for deep and creative insights into life? Or can that demand for clarity inhibit thought and involve damaging flaws of its own (as shown, for example, by Leiter's disregard for the hurt that he may cause)?

It is important to note again that the argument about clarity and obscurity draws its full force from an effect that Derrida's work is supposed to have, rather than on its inherent lack of clarity. It would matter little if that work were never read. It matters much more if it is read widely and has a lot of influence. This is in turn significant because it means that the criticism of Derrida's work is itself political, in the sense that it is arguing for a greater space for the work of the critics or of those they admire: a space that they claim has been falsely usurped.

The crux of the debate turns on the definition of thought in relation to its political role. If thought can always be clear in a well-defined way, and if that clarity is politically effective and on the side of justice and the good, then Derrida's critics have a strong point. But one of the main remarks made by poststructuralist thinkers is that thought is much more than a series of apparently clear propositions linked by valid arguments on premises we all agree upon. This does not mean that clarity is attacked as a bad thing. It means that clarity and accessibility are not sufficient conditions for defining thought.

For example, towards the latter part of his career, Derrida wrote a series of texts that were more autobiographical than his early works. These were not full autobiographies, but combinations of reflections on his life and experiences in relation to wider problems and questions. The books do not give us clear formulae or series of true propositions. Instead, they put forward series of interlinked ideas where themes such as language, identity and translation are explored in such a way as to allow us to understand their complexity and the stakes involved in the various simplifying claims about them.

One of these ideas, in *Le Monoliguisme de l'autre*, is that, in using a language to communicate, we depend on a promise that the languages we use will become one. This reduction of all languages to a single clear idiom is implied because we suppose that others will understand our communication and therefore we suppose that we shall share a language. The attempt to communicate is therefore a claim to bridge differences through the medium of the language; in language two become one. Many languages should therefore become one to increase the power of language to bridge difference and bring peace through understanding.

Derrida highlights the violence implied in this promise but also its messianic power. The demand for clarity is dangerous because clarity justifies violent judgements and exclusions on the basis of a promise of a world of understanding and togetherness (in a purely rational society, or one based on a common religion, or a commonly understood principle of tolerance). It would be a case of this violence to think that Derrida is simply opposed to this messianic power. Instead, he wants to draw our attention to it, not so that we turn away from the capacity of languages to become one, but to remind us of the exclusions and costs of this dream, of its necessary failures, but also of its basis in the feel and respect for otherness and for care. It should be listened to, but not followed unconditionally. This feel for the hidden promises and violence in even the soundest form of thought is one of the many important legacies of Derrida's work. It allows us to be more sensitive and ethical; to turn our backs on it due to an apparent difficulty is to lack both thoughtfulness and ethical sense.

three

Poststructuralism as philosophy of difference: Gilles Deleuze's *Difference and Repetition*

How do we take structuralism further?

In 1972 Gilles Deleuze published a short essay on structuralism, "How do we Recognize Structuralism?", for the twentieth-century volume of a multi-volume history of philosophy. It is probable that the essay was written some time earlier. In its opening paragraphs Deleuze situates it around 1967: near to the date of publication of his masterwork *Difference and Repetition* [*Différence et repetition*] in 1968. This dating is highly plausible, since the essay is very close to the earlier book in its concepts and arguments.

This essay on structuralism is very important for any work on poststructuralism and Deleuze because it shows how his work fits with structuralism, but also how it changes it and makes it more radical. The essay does not really answer its opening question: how do we recognize structuralism? Or at least it does not do so historically. Instead, Deleuze takes many of the philosophical arguments from *Difference and Repetition* and reflects on what structuralism can become and how radical it can be. The essay is therefore about poststructuralism as much as it is about structuralism. It is about structuralism in a very a radical guise.

The view of thought as the interpretation and transformation of what came before is typical of Deleuze's philosophy. He insists on the creative aspects of thought, because its role is to revivify structures that tend towards fixity. He sees fixity as defined by representation, that is, a form of repetition of the same. This explains why his book title includes repetition but together with difference. An affirmative repetition must be understood as the adding in of differences and variations to repetition.

Deleuze's philosophy is about repeating by rendering something different and by avoiding representation. He seeks to do this in the essay through the search for a radical structuralism. In *Difference and Repetition*, he does so through a critique of representation and of the role of identity in philosophy, for example, in the identity of the concept. He then insists on the creative role of thought in relation to signs of difference. These signs appear through intense sensations that determine intense ideas (although these should not be thought of as representations in a human mind, but as the conditions for actual evolutions and novelty).

For Deleuze, structure is not defined as a repetition of what the structure is about, as if the structure was a copy of the structure of an external object. Instead, and surprisingly, the structure is defined as a necessary condition for the transformation of the thing. For Deleuze, structure is not a theoretical model of a structured thing. It is the reason for the transformation and evolution of the thing. Poststructuralism, in a Deleuzian sense, is therefore the view that structure can be seen as the limit of the knowledge of a thing, where that limit is the condition for the evolution and living intensity of something. Structure is a living part of things. It is their intensity and the source of becoming and of change in them.

This is a counter-intuitive definition of structure, but Deleuze explains it powerfully in his essay. He is careful to show why structure must be about change rather than representation. The force of his explanation comes from the work done in *Difference and Repetition*. This makes the essay a good introduction to the poststructuralist side to Deleuze's work and in particular to his new definition of the sign and to his most important poststructuralist term: the simulacrum. The simulacrum is a sign of difference rather than identity. It is resistant to representation and invites us to repeat it in new ways.

In "How do we Recognize Structuralism?", structuralism is seen as an ongoing creative and interpretative process. Deleuze sees his work as part of that process (HRS: 192). In the final lines of the essay, he writes angrily about books that stand against things, leaving us in no doubt as to his positive attitude to structuralism. Neither structuralism nor poststructuralism is primarily against-X or essentially oppositional. This is also true for their relation. The latter must be seen as the transformation of the former away from the concept of representation and away from definitions of difference in terms of identity.

Deleuze highlights seven criteria for the recognition of structuralism in order to give his version of this transformation: the symbolic; locality or position; the differential and singular; differenciating and differenciation (these technical terms allow Deleuze to distinguish actual differences and the processes that lead to them from what he calls virtual differences and their processes, which are written "differentiation"); the serial; empty place; and the move from the subject to practice. These work well as quite general criteria but in each he also gives rather extreme versions of standard ideas. This is because each one is selected to allow strongly Deleuzian concepts to emerge. The connection to structuralism is made through series of key structuralist authors, such as Lévi-Strauss, and through series of carefully constructed examples. So the criteria allow for a general understanding of structuralism in relation to poststructuralism. Each criterion highlights what makes structuralism stand apart from what preceded it. Each also emphasizes important characteristics of Deleuze's poststructuralism as a radical development of structuralism. The reflection in terms of recognition is strange, in Deleuzian terms, since in *Difference and Repetition* he criticizes the faculty of recognition for giving a slanted and damaging "image of thought".

However, this is not a contradictory position because Deleuze is not really giving us criteria for the correct recognition of structuralism. Instead, he is giving us criteria for the creation of a line of thought consistent with structuralism. It seems as if he was asked to write an entry on structuralism for a work of history, but then decided to answer a different question, while using the original format. This different question is: in what way is your philosophy true to structuralism and yet a radical version of it? The answer is in terms of formal characteristics, rather than essential definitions, that is, Deleuze explains how things work, rather than what they are.

This focus on practice is also typical of Deleuze's version of poststructuralism and, indeed, of most poststructuralist works. They are a matter of practical and strategic transformation, with political and ethical goals. The question "What is this?" is always the wrong starting question from this point of view. We are always thrown into an ongoing series of tense transformations and stresses. The right question is how to transform and work with them: how to thrive with them as intensely as a situation allows, but with no certainties to fall back on.

The question of what things are must always be secondary to this insistence on the relation between thought and life as a struggle between re-energizing and de-intensifying forces. Deleuze's poststructuralism is strongly Nietzschean in its sense of life as will to power and as a strategic struggle between nihilism (as the loss of the will to value life) and chaos (as the collapse into a chaotic lack of determinacy). This connection was made explicit in Deleuze's influential book on Nietzsche, *Nietzsche and Philosophy* (1962).

The symbolic, position and locality

Deleuze's first criterion for the recognition of structuralism, the symbolic, follows an opening remark that structuralism is about language and not anything else. There is structure where there is language, rather than where there are things or minds. What this means is that we need differences that appear in the linguistic interaction between meaning and thing, before we can separate a structure from them. Otherwise, we could think in terms of things "as such" or ideas "as such", without having to refer to their structural relations.

Deleuze's point is that structure matters because it is something more than what we understand the objective thing to be, or what we imagine things to be. Instead, structure must be independent of those things, yet part of what makes them complete for thought. Language is what allows this independence, but also this constitutive role.

Structuralism is therefore not a matter of the relations that hold between the imaginary and the real. It is not about relating our imagination to real things. It is not about explaining how our minds and objects come to diverge, how they can be made to coincide, and why they sometimes come apart and sometimes work together. Instead, there is a symbolic realm that has nothing to do with symbols as something essentially connected to what we imagine and to what we perceive.

This move beyond reality and the imagination is crucial in understanding what structuralism and poststructuralism share. They are opposed to any privileging of the real as something that can be shown. They are opposed to any privileging of the imagination as a power held in relation to the real. *Deleuze's poststructuralism is not about what can be shown or what can be imagined about what can be shown. It is about searching for the structural conditions for the real and for imagination. It is about freeing thought from references to an illusory reality and to a limited human imagination.*

Instead, the symbol does not have the unity of the perceived "real" thing (it is not a well-defined representation). Nor does it have the internal division of the imagined thing (the distinction drawn between the image and what it is an image of). If it were either of these, then there would be no superior value to structure. It would merely be a form of reference, understood as a representing relation between what is imagined and what it should refer to. So the first step in freeing structuralism and poststructuralism from fixed meanings and references is to deduce a third term: structure.

The validity of such deductions and their grounds is one of the most problematic aspects of Deleuze's philosophy. It is important to keep in mind critical questions against his poststructuralism such as: "Why are these descriptions true?" and "Are these valid deductions?" To go beyond a view of poststructuralism as merely descriptive, it is important to understand the new kinds of philosophical argument and deductions introduced by *Difference and Repetition*.

The search for the criteria for the recognition of structuralism is a case of this method, since the criteria are not objective descriptions or the results of an empirical survey. Instead, they are deductions of the necessary conditions for the significance of a philosophy that concentrates on structure. These conditions start from the premise that structure has a value of its own. The point is then to explain the conditions for that value.

This approach allows the criteria to give a complex view of structure and of its relation to things and to imagination. It is a deduction of the significance of radical structuralism as something that goes beyond objectivity (the real object) and subjectivity (our imagination). But it is important to note that the deduction is only as good as the power of its premises, in the sense of how convinced we are that structure is significant in some special way. This does not mean that Deleuze's argument is circular and that the conclusion is also the premise. He is deducing a form of structure from its significance, rather than its significance from itself. This is typical of Deleuze's work: he tries to deduce the formal conditions for strategic action based on initial impulses or intensities. His work is transcendental in the sense outlined in the introduction to this book.

In poststructuralism, values and conditions are never identities (such as a commandment, "Taking a life is always wrong", or a logical rule, "A proposition is either true or false"). Instead, the values are pure movements (the varying intensities of sensations and affects) and the formal conditions are the necessary conditions for these movements: for their resistance to identification. You start "where you feel differently" and not "where you know the same as" or "follow the same rules or laws as". You then seek to find the conditions necessary for the resistance of that feeling to a return to identity and to sameness.

Deleuze answers the question "What is structure precisely – how does it constitute a third symbolic term?" with the deduction of the next criterion. Structure is about the symbolic, where the symbolic is a position or locality. This is not in the sense of a specific part of actual space (this would still be reference) or a specific part of the imagination (this would still leave symbols as imaginary) but as a state of the space of all relations.

Structuralism and poststructuralism work on relations, but these relations do not hold between things or ideas, but between different series of other relations. This explains the above claim about space, since the relations can be thought of as constructing a new space of their own, independent of related ideas or referents. What matters is not that A is related to B, but that the structure A–B is different from the structure A–B–C. So structure is not about symbols as something that can be perceived (a road sign) and that has a meaning ("Stop here"). It is about the symbolic as a process where the symbol implies a rearrangement of relations in structures (the new road sign as implying a changing set of symbolic relations with other signs and much wider).

Radical structuralism and poststructuralism are concerned with changes between different relations. They work on the relational conditions for the appearance of things we can refer to in language and for the things we can sense. Deleuze uses the term "transcendental" in this context, emphasizing that empirical work on actual differences presupposes prior structures of relations.

For example, within the structure made up of all words and all combinations of them, different human practices use different sets of words and relations between them. Structuralism is not primarily interested in how one given set of relations works (although this kind of empirical work is necessary). It is interested in what is at stake when a set of relations becomes distinguished from another (how a given set comes to be given and what is at stake when it is). This work is beyond empirical observation and moves into the detached observation of selections and omissions.

The turn to a highly technical set of structural relations and language, for example in the understanding of the human body and its sickness, is therefore a partial detachment from a wider set of relations, indeed, from all relations. From a philosophical point of view it is not primarily important to understand how the technical approach works and how its internal relations are structured. It is much more important to work with the shifts between structures, from emotions or religious structures to technique, for instance. Indeed, any point of view is incomplete without this extension (it is never enough to be merely technical, merely religious, merely artistic).

Detachment here refers to Deleuze's claim that meaning depends on a prior set of combinations of relations that themselves have no fixed meanings. Structuralists do not only note that something means something different. They note which changes in structures have been necessary for this meaning to emerge: "sense always emerges from the combination of elements that are not themselves signifying" (HRS: 175).

Deleuze claims this shift in topic as a condition for the move to the space of relations and away from the space of things (an objective world that can be referred to) and away from the space of the imagination (the mind). This new space does not allow for the kind of detachments available in others (in terms of individual objects and individual minds or ideas). Structural relations are complete in the sense that a relation is connected to all others. Therefore, when a given structure emerges it is only by focusing on some relations rather than others. But the "discarded" or "detached" relations are still there as a background for the selected ones.

When dealing with objects or imagined things, it is possible to think that we can consider them in the abstract: grasp an object or an imagined thing without having to take account of all others. With structural relations this is not possible. In pointing this out, Deleuze is bringing structuralism into a commitment to complete connectivity characteristic of his philosophy. His philosophy is of completeness, where the notion of a final truth about an abstract object in itself, or about a representation in itself, or about a particular content of the mind, is absurd. We are connected to all things and all things are in us, as we are in them.

A first consequence of this transcendental condition of complete connection, noted by Deleuze, is that there must always be an overproduction of sense, since any given space of relations is always a selection made in a wider one. There are always more combinations beyond those that have happened to be selected or highlighted in a given situation. This view is developed through his novel definitions of the sign and of sense in *Difference and Repetition* and *The Logic of Sense* (1969). Signs are multiple mobile structures of relations, rather than binary relations. Sense is not meaning; it is the disruption of identity in meaning and knowledge through sensation.

This overproduction means that sense emerges not against a background of non-sense (something like the existentialist absurd) but against an excess of sense due to the background of other combinations.

Although influenced by Sartre in his early years, Deleuze cannot be an existentialist. For him, life is not absurd, but endlessly complex.

This work on combinations determines a second consequence: structuralism's concern with games and play. Structuralism is interested in the way a given game allows for many different variations and plays. Each actual play is a chance-driven selection from a wider set. Deleuze links this to one of the most important statements from his philosophy: each life is always a chance-driven and creative selection – a dice-throw.

His poststructuralism is therefore committed to openness and opposed to determination. It is an anti-naturalism and an anti-determinism. So, where Deleuze still speaks of destiny, for example in *Difference and Repetition* or in *The Logic of Sense*, he does not mean a predetermined destiny. But nor does he mean a destiny within the control of a human free will. Instead, a destiny is to be connected to all things in a singular way that demands chance-driven selections and experimentations. Sometimes this means that Deleuze's philosophy is described as a higher empiricism, linking back to his early work on Hume, *Empiricism and Subjectivity* (1953). But the meaning of empiricism here is in terms of an open experimentation with a life rather than the specific and limited experiments of scientific empiricism.

In line with this distance from human free will, the formal aspects of games and structural relations imply a third consequence: structuralism cannot be a form of humanism. Deleuze's poststructuralism is opposed to humanism, in the particular sense of giving a fundamental priority to the human in any sense of values. This is because the structure that allows for the determination of the human and of human values starts with a selection of relations that is itself prior to the human. Deleuze says that structuralism "must be an anti-humanism". By this he does not mean that it is opposed to humanist values; rather, it is opposed to privileging those values as the foundation for thought.

Here, we can begin to see how Deleuze's account of structuralism is also an account of his version of what can also be called poststructuralism as a creative movement that stresses openness, play (in the sense already seen with Derrida) and an opposition to final or absolute truths or values. Deleuze has been able to do this by focusing on quite pure and formal aspects of structuralism, rather than on specific structures. He has asked the typically Deleuzian questions "How do structures emerge?" and "Under what conditions do they emerge?" in order to give a radical and very pure description of structuralism, in line with its later, most open and radical poststructuralist forms, including his own work.

Structures and reciprocal determination

Deleuze's move from a rigid structuralism to what we can call post-structuralism comes out even more strongly in the next criterion for "recognizing" structuralism. For Deleuze, structuralism explains the emergence of specific structural relations against a background of others. This emergence depends upon the reciprocal determination of relations by one another. A relation in a structure has no independent sense. It only appears because of its relation to others and because of their relation to it.

There are therefore only relations of reciprocal determination (A determines B, and B determines A) rather than relations where one side determines the other, but not the other way round. These latter relations are transcendent in the sense where the dominant relation transcends, rises above and maintains an independence from a lower one. Deleuze is wholly opposed to transcendence. Relations are always reciprocal and his philosophy is one of immanence: all things are connected in one world and nothing can claim to be external and superior.

Strictly differential relations are therefore described as pure differences, rather than as things with determinate meanings outside structures. They are only determined through relations with others and relations to actual things. Through the concept of reciprocal determination, Deleuze privileges the system or multiplicity of relations over its elements or individual relations. This means that he does not allow individual relations to have a recognizable identity, since this would give them a transcendent relation to the system or multiplicity.

Reciprocal determination between differences is perhaps the most important idea from *Difference and Repetition*. The fact that it appears in the structuralism essay is therefore very important in establishing continuity between structuralism and Deleuze's poststructuralism. We do not have a choice between different theories: structuralism or poststructuralism. The two are connected through shared conditions and each succeeds or fails in terms of how well it takes account of its conditions.

Deleuze's radical definitions of structuralism and structure are consistent with the definition of poststructuralism as the folding in of the limits of knowledge, where the limits are defined as pure differences. The structure is a limit made up of pure differences. A specific structure draws out a selection of relations and these in turn determine the significant points of the structure, that is, the points where the relations that have been selected meet.

Deleuze calls these significant points the singularities of the structure (his source for this term is mathematical). Singularities allow for the complete determination of the structure, beyond the relations, to the points where they come together. Singular points are important to Deleuze's version of radical structuralism (or poststructuralism) because they focus thought on points where relations and spaces change. What matters are the bifurcation points of a system, where it can be different and where selections can make it and have made it different. Once again, thought is not about essences or truths, but about evolutions, changes and differences.

Structure in radical structuralism is always a matter of pure differences, that is, variations between relations that are themselves only ever varying relations. These relations are given greater determinacy through the emergence of points where different structures meet: singularities. But, how can we recognize pure differences? How do they make sense for us? How do pure differences, variations and singularities interact with the world of objects and imagined things? In short, what is the connection between structure as rarefied condition and the world it is supposed to be a condition for?

To answer these questions Deleuze turns to further conditions or criteria for the recognition of structuralism. According to the fourth, differenciating and differenciation, a structure is real without being actual; that is, any structure as a space of relations could take up different actual forms. So a structure, although real "without being actual and ideal without being abstract", must be further determined through the actual forms that express it. That is, it must be expressed in actual identifiable forms.

Deleuze calls this process "actualization". Through it, ideal structural relations become expressed in actual parts and species. But, conversely, actual parts and species become connected to much wider structural relations. Deleuze claims therefore that the structure produces the actual. This means that the actual is incomplete when seen as independent from the structural selections required for a given structure to be related to a given set of species and parts.

This explains why his radical version of poststructuralism matters: we neither understand nor can create with actual things in a complete way unless we take account of the ideal structures they are related to. The selections and creations that have had to occur for a given species and set of parts, and the open set of other relations, are central to working with the evolution and future of actual things: "genesis, like time, goes from the virtual [the ideal] to the actual, from the structure to its actualization" (DR: 252).

This appeal to relations of reciprocal determination between struc- tures and between the ideal or virtual and the actual shows the demand- ing metaphysical nature of Deleuze's poststructuralism. He is the most inventive modern creator of new concepts and systems and he makes the most difficult claims for the reality of new and strange philosophical views of reality. In terms of this difficulty, it is helpful to see how these systems relate to more simple views of structure, as in his article on structuralism. It is also helpful to contrast Deleuze with Derrida and to note how both are concerned with pure difference and with the critique of identity. However, where deconstruction is always involved with the destruction of metaphysics and with its return, even in deconstruction Deleuze seems happier to construct a metaphysics more able to cope with the demands of radical philosophies of difference.

It would be a mistake, however, to oppose the two thinkers. This is because Deleuze never constructs a metaphysics based on origins and on presence in Derrida's sense. This explains why the former tries to define structuralism independently of an identified grounding reality or power of imagination. Equally, it is possible to think of Derrida's key terms within Deleuze's metaphysics, in particular where both try to work on the differential transcendental conditions for actual things. There are important subtle differences, but gross judgements about oppositions will always miss their significance.

Thus, for Deleuze, the virtual structure is never that of a human unconscious nor that of a human imagination. Both would set external limits on how structures could be combined. Structures are essentially problematic for Deleuze, in the sense where relations cannot be resolved according to a final logic that gives rules for their combination. Instead, structures involve contingent and tense, chance-driven, meetings that would be chaotic except for their relation to actual identifications that never resolve them as problems but move the problem along and give it temporary form. This means that his poststructuralism is opposed to logicism, but also to any programmatic or logical sense of total syntheses or trends. This is often referred to as its anti-Hegelianism, but that is far too crude and misses deep debts and complex differentiating relations.

Problems (not questions), series (not identities), synthesis (not abstraction)

Deleuze insists on the importance of the concept of the problem over and above the concept the question. This is a very important facet of poststructuralism that can be associated with many of its forms, since it shows the open-ended aspect of the movement. Problems, in the Deleuzian sense, are open-ended and continuous – in the sense that all problems are interrelated – whereas questions are curtailed by answers. These may demand new and different questions, but the original questions remain solved.

Poststructuralism is opposed to grounding truths and to final goals (or even directions). This opposition requires a different mode of thought from questions demanding answers. The turn to problems is explained by the demand to move things on but not to resolve them. Do not ask "What is this?", "What is best?", "Where shall we go?", or "What is the good?". Ask "Why are these questions irresolvable?", "What kinds of complex problems do they presuppose?", "What tensions and paradoxes are in play here?", and "How am I determined to move the problem on?". As to the questions "Why should there be any movement?" and "What determines a problem in the first place?", Deleuze answers both through two further criteria in the recognition of poststructuralism. A problem is determined through the serial relations of structures, that is, by the way in which different structures meet and clash.

There is no structure without such meetings, since structures are always selections from all others. However, those selections set up differences that raise problems as to how the structures are related at all. Problems are defined by the way structures do not fit together and yet have internal drives to achieve that fit. If there are structures conditioning both actual reality and imagination, then there must be problems, since otherwise the structures would fall back on to one or the other.

It is helpful to view this in concrete terms, for example, through the example of a clash of cultures. According to the poststructuralist view, the clash between two cultures defines both, but both are also driven to resolve the clash (even a violent reaction is still a drive to some sort of resolution). However, poststructuralist thinkers want to cure us of the thought that there could be a final resolution (however peaceful). This is because irresolvable structural problems are the condition for the evolution of living things and systems.

The best we can do is move tensions and blockages on and use them as creative opportunities to reinvigorate life, free of the illusion that one day, thanks to the right truths, all will come to be peaceful, or at least settle in a trend towards peace. This illusion is the source of a form of violence proper to thought that all poststructuralist thinkers seek to avoid, but on different bases and through different methods.

This does not imply that poststructuralism, as characterized by Deleuze, is a form of relativism. There are principles for selections both in the resistance to identification (and hence to forms of racism or nationalism, for example) and in the demand to connect rather than divide (and hence to a demand to always seek where we are connected to others through sensations and structures). This is not a philosophy of "anything goes" (as we shall also see with Foucault, later). It is not a nihilistic philosophy based on indifference. Quite the contrary: it is a philosophy of *always resist false representations and final limited truths* and *never see a difference as a difference between essential identities*. It is also a philosophy of *seek out the intense connections that relate you to the lives of others* and *intensify those relations*. It is commitment to principles such as *avoid the violence implied by the negation of other values* and *experiment with ways of expressing connections that have become dormant.*

Far distant from the irresponsibility of a caricatured relativism (which says something about the need for such caricatures in weak systems of thought), Deleuze's philosophy challenges us to find a way through problems. This way is guided by affirmative principles regarding intense connections and secondary principles regarding the avoidance of false representations. He calls the latter stupidity.

So, when Deleuze privileges problems over questions, the point is to show us how thought is a way of finding a singular path through a series of tensions that we are thrown into. To think in terms of questions, such as "What is the absolutely right thing to do?", is inconsistent with the demand to avoid final representation (including those that would be implied by such absolute rights, for example, in the notion of an absolute evil opposed to that right.)

Problems are also determined, however, by the objects that participate in the expression or actualization of each structure. This is because different structures have to be related in the actual, if they are also related as ideal or virtual. It is also because a merely virtual or structural problem lacks specificity and is chaotic until it is expressed in a given situation. A problem is not complete until it has been rendered specific and determined according to actual parts.

In effect, there is no virtual or ideal problem until it is a problem for an actual situation. The problem would not matter without actual sensations that it conditioned and that expressed it. We can think of this in terms of an analogy with the relation between a theoretical model and practical applications of it. The model for the stresses in bridges lacks something until it is applied in the construction of specific bridges. In

Deleuzian terms, there is a reciprocal determination between the model and application, as the model is changed to reflect practical experiences and as the practice is guided by the model.

But the way ideal problems and actual expressions of them are related cannot resolve their differences. It is for this reason that Deleuze draws our attention to a further deduction of the sixth criterion: the empty place. Structuralism must operate with the notion of an empty place through which different structures pass. The place must be empty, otherwise it would either not fit with one or other of the structures or it would collapse the difference between them. Structuralists therefore depend on defining, or rather creating, this empty place or object ("object=x"). By circulating within different structures and between them, it allows ideal structures and actual expressions of them to come together and to gain an energizing difficulty (in the sense of raising tensions and problems that demand actual expressions but that also curtail final practical resolutions).

Deleuze argues that the object or place is necessarily a cause for interpretation and creativity. This is because its emptiness needs to be filled, in the sense that when we encounter something without meaning we seek to determine what it means. Yet, in this case, that meaning cannot be objective or defined from within any given system, because it relates different structures to one another.

If there were a final rule and objectivity for determining the object, then that rule would determine a superstructure for the resolution of problems and for bringing structuralism back, once more, to the opposition between actual reality and the imaginary. So the object=x is created or interpreted not in terms of its internal meaning, but rather in the way it is related to further structures and situations.

Deleuze's poststructuralism is about adding structures and creating expressions around difficult and puzzling actual "objects" and in terms of ideal problems. The object=x or empty place is therefore related to individuals and to their different ways of reacting to and creating with the object. Indeed, Deleuze uses the term "empty place" to avoid having to use the term "object", since this would already overdetermine it and privilege certain structures (ones linked to notions of objectivity and knowledge, for instance).

For example, take a disputed piece of land struggled over by competing claims that cannot be rendered consistent with one another. This land has a status as an empty place or object=x. It takes on different significances for different structures and situations. Deleuze's philosophy is about the creation of new ways of putting the land into structures so that a blocked conflict is moved and opened up. It is not a matter of resolving the conflict, and even less a matter of deciding in favour of one side or the other. It is a matter of introducing new sensations and ideas that move both sides beyond a deepening opposition caused by strengthening opposed representations. Of course, there can be no guarantees of success, let alone perpetual peace. Yet, by opening up the situation, by forcing stultifying and exclusive identifications to give way, Deleuze's poststructuralism can be a powerful force for political change.

This creative opening need not be thought of in artistic terms. In his work for the *Groupe Informations Prisons* with Michel Foucault, Deleuze's political action involved looking for new ways for prisoners to seek redress for overt and covert forms of repression in prisons. For instance, by bringing released prisoners together with ones still in detention, the group allowed them to make public the actions of particular prison guards in ways that were not possible before (since the guards had the power for further retribution for those still under their control, but had no such power over the others). Or it could be thought in psychoanalytic terms through the work of Jacques Lacan, where a similar move beyond traditional poststructuralism is achieved through a study of the object in relation to the libido and to the unconscious (see Chapters 4 and 6, on Lyotard and Kristeva).

The key to the political action on prisons was to break down the simple divisions around prison discourse and actual and ideal structures (inside/outside; innocent/guilty; outlaw/state official; wrongdoer/guard) in order to allow for new ways to express the wrongs implied by them. For example, meetings were organized where prisoners, guards, families of prisoners, doctors and activists were brought together. Such meetings forced established ways of thinking and acting to come out in the open and face challenges in new ways: "Something new is happening in prisons and around prisons" (WPU: 285).

Contesting the identity of the subject

The empty place or object=x in actual structures and its relation to ideal ones leads to a final condition for radical structuralism and for Deleuze's poststructuralism. The absence of final control of that puzzling place and its relation to ideal problems is a challenge to the founding notion of the subject.

The subject of knowledge and action – the knower and doer – is destabilized through its relation to empty places and to events that draw it in but that resist its understanding. There are sensations that transmit a sense of significance; we feel that they are important. But these sensations are also barriers to satisfactory identification; we cannot fully understand that importance.

This challenge works for established knowledge when presented with limit cases that it cannot handle; here is something we cannot account for. But it also works for recognized methods for acquiring new knowledge. For methods, the limit case is a challenge to the form of the method, rather than to the state of knowledge it has at a given time; here is something that we could not understand without changing our views of truth. However, it is very important to avoid a serious misinterpretation at this point. It is also important to realize that misinterpretations are possible, due to the tight deductions and arguments put forward by Deleuze. His philosophy is not an invitation to create freely in terms of its own interpretation (or anything else, for that matter).

The remarks on the subject have nothing to do with eliminating the subject or claiming that we can go beyond the subject once and for all. They are not about an opposition to the subject, but about realizing that its claim to be a foundation for truth (in knowledge) or for action (through free will) are illusory. This is why Deleuze speaks of contesting the identity of the subject, rather than having done with it:

> Structuralism is not at all a thought that eliminates the subject, but a thought that shatters it and systematically distributes it. It is about a thought that contests the identity of the subject, that dissipates it and forces it to move from place to place, an always nomadic subject, made of individuations, but impersonal ones, or singularities, but pre-individual ones.   (HRS: 267)

This passage sums up many of the most significant aspects of Deleuze's radical approach to structuralism and to his own take on what we can call poststructuralism. (He never uses the term in the essay on structuralism. Indeed the term, although existing before the 1960s, had little currency until much later in the 1980s.)

It is important to see that Deleuze does not call structuralism a method, or form of knowledge, but "a thought". This is his way of insisting that it is a living practice, with loose conditions but no established fixed rules or body of knowledge. It has transcendental conditions and characteristic conditions, but these do not give it a fixed identity. Secondly, there is no elimination of the subject, but its systematic distribution: that is, the subject is set in different and incommensurable structures (structures with no common rule, norm or measure). This setting means that the subject must be mobile. The subject is not capable of finally collecting or bringing its setting together into final order. Instead, the subject is compelled to follows its dispersion: drawn into a nomadic existence, rather than capable of measuring and charting the spaces around it.

This nomadic subject is not universal but radically individuated according to the different ways structures and "empty places" take hold of it. So it is no longer the case that subjects can be brought together under the banner of a same knowledge or capacity for knowledge or free will. Instead, they are loosely related through structures that draw on each one of them in different ways. This explains why individuations must be impersonal, since otherwise the definition of "person" would provide an overarching basis for comparing individuation: we would all be different, but as persons. The same holds for singularities, that is, the intense points that attach us to different ideal structures. They cannot be understood in terms of a full definition of a human individual, because then the definition of human would cross structures and reduce their differences. Singularities would no longer be prior and determining.

Deleuze's poststructuralism is therefore a radical way of thinking about individuation and singularities. Sensations, intensities and changes in structures make each of "us" an individual, and not an individual person of human being, or subject. Each individual is the whole of the world under a singular perspective, rather than a subset of the group of human beings or persons. Sensations are feelings that go beyond fixed shared perceptions. Instead, they are individual relations to events that cannot be directly related to others.

Intensities are the degrees of those sensations as they relate to actual structures: how those structures are differently significant for each individual. We can think of this as saying that different events are intense in different ways for each of us; for example, in the way a scene leads to a variety of different reactions, but also in the way that each participant feels a barrier to complete expression of its difference to the others.

These differences demand a new politics and ethics, since they force us to move beyond notions of shared intersubjective norms and values. They also force us to move beyond notions of perfect communication or shared significant truths. This is not to deny that there are norms and values, truths and communications. It is to deny that these have a determinant foundational role to play. They are not the basis on which ethics and political action should be constructed.

Instead, Deleuze argues that structuralist politics is a matter of resisting two "accidents" that can occur in structures. First, there is the risk of the empty space becoming detached from individuals, that is, that actual situations lose their intensity and lose the drives that move them on and relate them to problems. This is the challenge of nihilism. Once negative actual situations become viewed as necessary they become the cause of despair. We then face the danger of losing any sense of values, that is, sensations, that drive us to experiment with the situation in its relation to ideal problems. Secondly, there is the risk of the empty space becoming overly identified across situations and structures. This would imply that a single illusory set of beliefs and system of knowledge would dominate all others, thereby leading to a false orthodoxy. Poststructuralism is always resisting this risk, due to its commitment to ongoing structural differences as conditions for actuality.

In reaction to these two inevitable dangers, Deleuze defines radical structuralism or poststructuralism as a creative practice that is always geared to the mutation of actual situations in their relation to ideal structures. Poststructuralism is a practice of permanent revolution:

> This point of mutation precisely defines a praxis, or rather the place where praxis should become installed. Since structuralism is not only inseparable from the works that it creates, but also from a practice in relation to the products that it interprets. Whether this practice be therapeutic or political, it designates a point of permanent revolution, or permanent transfer.
>
> (HRS: 191)

Deleuze's essay on structuralism is a sign of this revolution. It explains why the essay finishes with remarks about transformation, since, in a sense, he is guiding us beyond the question "How do we recognize structuralism?" to the question "Whither structuralism now, with which intensities, for this individual?"

This also explains why Deleuze's work is resistant to any final distinction between structuralism and poststructuralism, since such a division would deny the openness of the situations and structures and the power to transform them without introducing oppositions and discontinuities. We have to use the terms "structuralism", "radical structuralism", "poststructuralism", or other terms that risk identifications. But, for Deleuze, the terms should be resisted when they begin to fix thought.

The simulacrum

There are at least two further sources for an understanding of Deleuze's development of structuralism into poststructuralism. The first is his reflection on the sign in the works on Proust, *Proust and Signs* [*Proust et les signes*] (1964 and 1970 – with additional material). The second is his development of the sign in *Difference and Repetition* through a new concept of the sign associated with the simulacrum. Both books respond to questions left hanging in the essay on structuralism. What new theory of the sign must we have in order to account to for the mobility and transformations implied by Deleuze's definition of structure as pure variation in relation to actualization? What justification can there be for such theories?

In the preface to *Difference and Repetition*, Deleuze begins to answer these questions by opposing two senses of repetition: the repetition of the same and repetitions of difference. In the former, repetition is secondary to identity and a thing is said to be repeated if the same thing can be identified in different places. In the latter, repetition is a variation in a series, where the variation is itself resistant to identification.

This distinction leads to two different senses of difference: difference as a difference between identities and difference as pure variation (or difference in itself – to avoid prior definitions of purity). The challenge of Deleuze's philosophy is to see identity as a necessary but incomplete part of reality dependent on deeper series of variations of differences: "Identities are only simulated, produced as an optical 'effect' by a deeper play, that of difference and repetition" (DR: 1).

However, this means that familiar grounds for structuralism and, indeed, for wider common-sense views of reality, must be replaced as false. The sign cannot be a relation between an identified signifier (a perceived identity) and a represented meaning (a meaning in a mind or accessible to minds). The sign must be something else, a simulacrum: "In the simulacrum, repetition is already repetition of repetitions and difference is already difference of differences" (DR: 2). In the preface, Deleuze gives a helpful broad example for this shift from identity to variation. He describes an opposition between the repetition of the same in daily life through mechanical reproduction and our efforts to restore small variations and modifications within them. We can see such variations in the window boxes and curtains of vast modern blocks. Each resident resists the sameness of repeated identical windows by attempting to give an individual stamp to the same reproduced space.

The challenge for Deleuze, however, is to show how this individual stamp is not a more minute representation and sameness (in the perception of a represented pattern and its meaning or in the identity of particular flowers and planting patterns and their meaning). This is what the concept of the simulacrum tries to do: to say that a sign is not a relation between identities, but an intense individual sensation associated with a movement within all actual identities and with variations within all virtual or ideal structures. So in the example of the windows it is not the fact that there are identifiable differences that matters. Instead, it is what these express about unidentifiable variations in the sensations and ideas of the individuals involved in the creation and experience of the varied windows. For Deleuze, each identifiable variation is a signal for much deeper processes. The simulacrum is the synthesis, the coming together, of the signal and the processes.

The simulacrum cannot itself be represented, since this would once again subject difference to identity. Instead, Deleuze speaks of the complete simulacrum, rather than the whole one. A thing can be thought of as complete, that is, thought of in terms of all the processes that it brings together. But that does not mean that we can have a full representation of the whole thing. We have a sense of the thing and a set of guidelines or diagrams as to what it synthesizes and how. But this does not mean that we can grasp the thing as a whole and in all its parts.

The concept of the simulacrum is developed further in two key parts of *Difference and Repetition*: at the end of the chapter on difference and at the end of the chapter on repetition. This is significant in so far as it shows how the concept brings together all the aspects of Deleuze's argument and how it is central to his philosophy. In the first part, Deleuze begins by criticizing Plato for defining the simulacrum as a fall away from the thing in itself. For Plato, the simulacrum is a copy, a representation, a lesser identification of a full identity. For Deleuze, there is no such full identity as condition for copies. This leads into a well-known clarion call of his poststructuralism: to reverse Platonism. This does not mean to overthrow it but to "deny the primacy of the original on the copy, of the model on the image" (DR: 92).

For Deleuze's poststructuralism, signs are not "signs for" or "signs of" something outside a system of signs. Signifiers are not primarily signifiers of a more important meaning. That meaning is not primarily a meaning for a more important object, or a meaning to be referred to a chain of meanings leading to ultimate truths. Instead, there are only copies and signs, free of any external reference to ultimate objects or meanings. Such copies are simulacra, that is, variations on other simulacra or differences running through series of other differences. For poststructuralism – in the sense of a structuralism that comes after ultimate senses of reality or meaning – we should "glorify the reign of simulacra and reflections" (DR: 92) rather than the abstract realm of forms or pure ideas.

Here, Deleuze rejoins Derrida's and Foucault's critiques of the origin. There is no origin, only an eternal chain of interconnected simulacra. Nothing exists outside such chains. Which means that everything depends on its repetition and has no independent reality outside that repetition: "everything exists only in returning, copy of an infinity of copies that allow no original, nor even an origin, to subsist" (DR: 92). Deleuze expresses this idea in terms of a special version of Nietzsche's doctrine of eternal return: everything returns, but only as different and only as variation. So the same never returns. Only difference returns. This means that Nietzsche's doctrine viewed as a moral lesson (if the same life returns eternally, you had better make it one worth living) is transformed into a view about reality (the real can only be variations or series of variations and identity is only a passing illusion).

This offers a very powerful resolution of the paradoxes and contradictions of Nietzsche's doctrine. If only the same returns, then how can it make sense to see eternal return as a moral lesson? But if I were to change my behaviour, that would imply a change in what returned eternally, which would contradict the initial premise. So Deleuze adds that it is never the same that returns, but difference, in its relation to a sameness that never returns. Furthermore, that returning difference cannot itself be identifiable, since then a version of the same would still return. So only pure difference can return.

This highly metaphysical work can seem quite abstract. But it is the heart of Deleuze's work in *Difference and Repetition*. First, it is the key explanation for the relation of difference to sameness in repetition. Secondly, it provides an explanation of the role of creation in Deleuze's philosophy of time and a way out of linear concepts of time (through the very special circularity of eternal return). Thirdly, the definition of the simulacrum has far-reaching consequences for a sense of Deleuze's poststructuralism as practice. We only rise to the challenge of reality when we seek to introduce variations into sameness. Life must be creative and experimental if it is to retain the intensity of the return of differences into sameness.

Poststructuralism is inconsistent with linear notions of time because they privilege an external sense of time as a line within which events have to take place. For poststructuralism events have effects that spread through time, forwards and backwards and in indivisible waves of reciprocal determination, rather than as successions of instants with causal relations to one another.

Deleuze's version of eternal return supports this critique of linearity and puts forward a counter-view based on the eternal (and not on the infinite). When we create we cut into linear time, by allowing the return of a difference that throws some given sameness away, never to return. There is an order of time through the sameness that can never return. Things will never be the same after each creation.

But creation also assembles what came before and after that cut through the relations of the returning difference to all other variations of differences. All differences and intensities return when we create. Time is therefore not only an order, but also an assembly. This cannot be true for linear time, where the past must be radically different and separate from the future. However, this assembly cannot be a whole, in the sense of a represented whole or even in the sense of a measurable progress or trend. Instead, because pure difference returns, time is also an opening on to an undetermined future, a radical cut that invites further creations and bans none in principle (other than those that dream of the repetition of the same).

Poststructuralism is sometimes characterized as a weak form of thought, lacking in rigour and philosophical depth, but Deleuze's philosophy shows that such statements are deeply ignorant. For example, his philosophy of time is a subtle and consistent development of our view of time that avoids many of the traditional paradoxes of traditional linear views of time. Time must be thought of as ordered, assembled and radically cut, rather than merely as any one of these.

Deleuze's commitment to creation based on this philosophy of time has deep ethical ramifications in insisting that we must find the variations in our lives and seek to vary them further. We should resist the temptations of sameness ("Who am I?", "What do I want to be?") and embrace those of difference ("Where am I becoming?", "Where can further becoming be put into play?"). There is a strong sense of freedom here, but not as free will. It is a freedom in relation to the return of differences, where freedom cannot be a relation to a simple openness or void, but to well-determined variations. This explains why Deleuze emphasizes connection and immanence (that all simulacra are in the same world and that there is nothing outside that world). It also sets up a powerful ethical and political opposition with thinkers that have to posit voids, gaps and an outside in order to ground a politics and an ethics based on freedom.

For Deleuze, we must always create within the repeating cycles of difference and disappearing sameness that we are thrown into. We are determined by the individual way in which the same is destroyed for us.

We can determine that way in a chance-driven and incomplete manner in the way our creations invite different variations to return and to resist identities.

It is interesting to see how far this position is at odds with standard definitions of postmodern art and philosophy. Although it is true of all the poststructuralist thinkers considered here, Deleuze is perhaps the best philosopher to show how poststructuralism has nothing to do with postmodernism in its most familiar definition of fragmentary works and ideas. At its worst, "postmodern" means fragments of identifiable bits resistant to the idea of a whole. Following Deleuze, at its best, poststructuralism means infinite connections of variations that resist identification. In this sense, poststructuralism is absolutely modern, but where modern means seeking completeness without sameness, without totality and without a representation of the whole.

The sign as event for thought

Structuralism and many other scientific approaches to language and to life maintain an external relation to their topic. They are modes of thought as "thinking on" rather than "thinking with". Deleuze explains and justifies a different approach through his work in *Difference and Repetition*.

Since all things are connected, but in terms of relations of reciprocal determination within actual things and within ideal ones – and most importantly between the two – there cannot be a true form of external thought, since there is no ground for it to rest upon. Poststructuralism is both anti-foundational and a new constructive way of thinking after the fall of all foundations (and with the inescapable risk of their return).

The place where we start to think in this new way is an event : an event for thought. It cannot be a foundation and Deleuze's philosophy cannot rest on such a foundation. Instead, he has to "dramatize", or enact, or express such an event. Only then can he begin the long chains of deductions that provide the rich form of his philosophy. This is why his philosophy can also be described as a transcendental empiricism: it begins with an experiment (a drama) and only then deduces a complicated structure of interconnected conditions.

One of the most interesting examples of this enactment, in the context of work on poststructuralism and the sign, is the conclusion to his *Proust and Signs*. There, using Proust as the dramatic entrance into a feel for what he means by sign, Deleuze explains how his work must be a new way of thinking about the sign and about thought:

Thought is forced to occur by the sign. The sign is the object of an encounter; but it is precisely the contingency of the encounter that guarantees the necessity of what it leads to think. The act of thought does not follow from a simple natural possibility. It is, on the contrary, the only true creation. Creation is the genesis of the act of thought in thought itself. Yet this genesis implies something that does violence to thought, that tears it from its natural stupor, from its merely abstract possibilities. To think, is always to interpret, that is, to explain, to develop, to decode, to translate a sign.   (PS: 190)

This means that for Deleuze's poststructuralism it is not possible to separate sign and thought. Like Proust's reminiscences, chains of thought begin with chance encounters. This is necessary, because thought is a relation to something unexpected and because, where thought is not jogged out of what it already known, there is no true thinking.

So the necessity that Deleuze speaks of is the necessary sensation that thought has radically strange and different limits: things that are both essential to what thought is and resistant to whatever it can know (its simple natural possibility as knowledge). This implies that thought must be a creative practice rather than a body of knowledge. But this also means that thought cannot be limited in its form rather than its content. We can no more have a definition of how thought must proceed, than have a store of all the truths that can properly be thought. Instead, thought is always about creating what it is, rather than falling back on what it has been and how it can develop (its natural stupor and abstract possibilities).

So without this strange trigger and enticement that happens to it, thought cannot develop from within. But this trigger, the sign, cannot be fixed according to a specific definition. That is why Deleuze's thought must go beyond structuralism, if structuralism works with a set definition of the sign. Such a definition is a limit on what thought can be and what signs can put it in motion.

Deleuze's philosophy is therefore to go beyond what we think interpretation, explanation, development and translation are. They must become something different in order to allow us to think with signs: defined as events where difference occurs. In *Difference and Repetition* he calls this going beyond, or transcending, the boundaries of given faculties of thought (an idea that we can also find in Foucault).

It is exciting to reflect on what kind of university and society this poststructuralism leads to in its opposition to the privileging of bodies of knowledge, faculties of thought or of the mind, and prior subject-specific definitions of signs and objects. Here are some possible temporary ideas (always to be reviewed, but not with the overly simple logic of simply negating them):

- Thinking must seek out ways to be jogged by radically different experiences.
- Faculties and disciplines should be resolutely interdisciplinary.
- Universities and disciplines, forms of writing and specialities, should be practical, not in the sense of a divided theory and practice, but in the sense where there is no theory without prior practice.
- All laws, rules and guidelines should be open to challenge, not in the sense of the formal possibility of questioning them, but in the sense of experimenting with ideas and practices that raise the possibility of working in a radically different way.
- Thought should be open to sensation, not in the sense of well-determined perceptions, but in the sense of limit-sensations (in art and literature, for example).
- Thought should be given space to encounter contingent events: space away from accountancy and accountability.
- All forms of established common sense and common values should be criticized and tested.

These may sound extreme, but they are not. Each is a relation between the known and its limits, not a repudiation of the known at all. Each is for thought, rather than against it. If these principles are against anything it is stupidity, entrenchment, corruption and complacency in thought (and hence in universities and societies).

Poststructuralism is not extreme, in the sense of wanting to go to some wild anarchic promised land; rather, it wants to release the possibilities of thought from the inadequacies of restricted images: "A thought that is born within thought, an act of thought engendered within its own genealogy, neither given through innateness, nor presupposed in reminiscence, is a thought without image" (DR: 217).

four

Poststructuralism as philosophy of the event: Jean-François Lyotard's *Discours, figure*

Poststructuralism, aesthetics and events

Jean-François Lyotard's poststructuralism is distinctive due to its empha-sis on aesthetics and on art. He seeks to introduce aesthetic events into structures, subjects and objects. Structure is infused with emotion and a troubling materiality. *Wherever the detachment of structure is relied upon, Lyotard injects feelings associated with art and with other felt events* (a political act or feeling, a use of language, a passionate caress, a burst of enthusiasm).

Events are important because they undermine and transform lin-guistic structures and their relations to things. Aesthetic events, such as the feelings associated with artworks – the events of an encounter with art – also transform and are part of things. This means that there is no independent reality. There are transforming relations between matter, feelings and language (structure). These transformations are events. They can be forgotten, hidden, repressed or ignored, but they are there at work, nonetheless.

Lyotard does not believe that language or discourse, a connected subset of language, can capture events. Instead, deeply felt encounters show the structures of discourses to be insufficient for accounting for events. More profoundly, discourses depend on feelings and on the disturbance they cause. There is no discourse without the intensity of feelings.

Language and discourse owe their significance and evolution to events, defined as relations between feelings and matter. It is not about what you know about love, or even about what that knowledge allows you to do. It is about love-events, their shaping of knowledge, and the way they always escape the net that knowledge or subsequent decisions throw over them.

So, for Lyotard, crude versions of structuralism and the hold of structure on knowledge have to be deconstructed in favour of an openness to events. If structure is viewed as objective and independent of transformations linked to events, then it involves a false representation of reality. There is no cold structural theory with a truthful grasp of properties of objects. There is a complex of emotion-laden interactions.

This deconstruction does not aim to have finished with structure; he does not believe that this is possible. It aims to loosen structures, invite them to change and bring what was defined as other and intractable into play. In this sense, Lyotard's deconstruction must be seen as highly creative and transforming (this explains why he often shies away from the term "deconstruction", fearing a negative interpretation as destruction or critique).

Lyotard's *Discours, figure* is between Derrida's deconstruction and Deleuze's difference and repetition. It takes the practice of working within texts to open them up from the former. It takes the creative and metaphysical side of the latter. Together, they underpin one of the most underrated and rich texts of poststructuralism.

The mistrust of independent structures holds true for the referent of any discourse: the object associated with a structure, or thing in itself, or nature. These things do not exist independently of structure or of events. There is no brute object, reality or nature to be structured. Instead, we have processes where a posited object or referent is associated with energizing and transforming aesthetic events and with dynamic relations of interconnected structures.

For Lyotard, an object or referent changes with the feelings, desires and language that are associated with it. None of these can be separated from the others. However, where there are questions concerning change and values, feelings and desires should be privileged. This privilege cannot be extended to a full independence. Rather, events bring discourse and matter together in processes of transformation and new significance.

For example, an object of desire such as a body part cannot be separated from the economic, social and sexual discourses about it. A pierced brow or a smooth knee is not a neutral attractor for a natural desire. They cannot be separated from what has been and what can be said about them. However, despite this necessary attachment to discourse, the deep truths about the part, its power to move us, are revealed in events and through feelings. The curl across a forehead or the shaven base of a head go beyond what is said of them in events that reveal their deeper and individual significance.

The sense that emerges from the connection between the part and language only matters because of the new emergent desires and feelings. These demand change in discourses and imply change in their relations to the object. The event of a sexual or political desire, associated with a particular body part or material, changes everything. It introduces new and troubling senses into the world (for example, through counter-cultural fashion, politics and music). No objects and discourses are immune or safe from such disturbing events.

A possible contradiction appears at this point: how can Lyotard speak of matter or objects in relation to feelings and events and yet deny an independent external reality, referent, or object? The answer draws out one of the most original aspects of his thought and sensibility. For him, matter is prior to ideas, but not to feelings. Equally though, feeling is prior to language, but not to matter.

This intertwining of matter and feeling, according to relations of mutual transformation, is one of the most exciting and different aspects of Lyotard's thought. It bears strong relations to Deleuze's concept of reciprocal determination, to the point where it is possible to see Deleuze's metaphysics as consistent with Lyotard's aesthetics. The relation of matter and feeling also explains why Lyotard has been interested in the notion of events, but also why his notion of event is surprisingly different from common-sense views. An event is not something that happens to someone, understood, for example, as seeing something happen in a detached manner: A sees B. On the contrary, an event is a transformation into inseparable things, in the sense where they appear in a new way with the event: (A) and (B) become (A'B').

This difference is important because it stresses essential connections over distinctions, and because it characterizes connection in a particularly strong way. It is not a connection between two things but a fusing of them in an ongoing transformation. Furthermore, there is no internal reason why this fusing is not open to further transformations and external connections: (A'B') is already transforming into (A'B'C') and it will not stay still for you, as you struggle to keep hold of it, or hold it back.

Matter and feeling allow Lyotard to think about this meld as something that still involves differences. Matter is not only feeling and vice versa. They are inextricable in terms of the event, but they have different relations to further entities: to things, objects and nature, in the case of matter; and to thoughts, ideas and language, in the case of feelings (or sensations, depending on the period of Lyotard's works and on different translations of the French *sentiments*).

Lyotard's poststructuralism can therefore be thought of with greater precision as the turn away from ways of thinking that cannot do justice to the following points:

- truth is primarily a matter of events and only secondarily of correspondence or of consistency;
- events are complexes of feeling and matter, where neither of these must be identifiable in terms of an independent existence;
- dualist views of reality (subject–object, sense–reference, structure–reality) miss the essential intertwining of matter and feeling in events;
- knowledge defined in terms of such dualism and in terms of correspondence or consistency cannot grasp the event;
- art and philosophy must turn towards the event, not in exclusion of other things, but together with them.

If structuralism is defined (no doubt too simply in many cases) as the search for objective truths through abstract structures, then Lyotard's philosophy must be opposed to structuralism. This philosophy is perhaps more extreme than Deleuze's and Derrida's views, in not working with structuralism, except as one example of the structures of thought that have to be worked with and also resisted.

If this resistance is to be given a unifying formula, it is as follows. *Of the many systems of truth available to us, only one grasps the power of intense events: there is an essential relation of feeling and of the ungraspable openness of matter – we can only do justice to it by responding to events without fully objectifying or representing them.*

Against totality and for incommensurability

To understand the impact and significance of the above formula, it is helpful to follow three of its most important consequences. First, although structures of discourse, or positions, are interconnected, they can never be reduced to a single overarching system. This is because events show the limits of discourses and, in particular, the limits they present to one another. For Lyotard, these limits are absolute. There is no account of the differences between positions that can do full justice to them as they are revealed through events. Structuralism can be seen as leading to truths that can become the basis for relating different positions around them. He tries to show that there are differences that cannot be resolved in this way.

In one of his most influential and important books, *The Differend* (1988), Lyotard develops the concept of the differend in order to explain irresolvable differences between incommensurable positions. By incommensurable he means that the two positions have no common measure and can never have a common measure. A feeling, the feeling of the sublime, an unbreakable combination of pleasure and pain, or attraction and repulsion, is the sign of this impossibility. We feel that any resolution of a dispute would have to do some tort or damage to at least one of the sides.

The bond between attraction and repulsion in feelings is crucial to Lyotard, since it explains how his philosophy is a response to nihilism (to the loss of the will to resist, to value and to affirm). Yet it is also a response to the will to reduce differences to sameness in structures. One side of the feeling – the repulsion and pain – halts the desire to reduce to identity. The other side – the attraction and pleasure – still drives us towards a worthy response to this barrier. The event tears us apart and presents an insurmountable barrier, but this does not lead to despair. There remains the desire to do justice to the value of this barrier as resistance to false identifications.

Secondly, for Lyotard notions of the energy and intensity of feelings become very important in our relations to things (including complex things such as political or historical cases). This means that they become different for different spectators according to different feelings and intensities. There is no common reference point outside these intensities, although they may be shared, but not necessarily, and with no guarantee of permanence or perfect fit.

Earlier than *The Differend*, in his book *Libidinal Economy* (1974), Lyotard constructs a metaphysics of intensities hidden within structures. The intensities are capable of altering the structures and transforming them. They occur where structures meet each other and where intense feelings are released as disruptive events; for example, in the way an emotion flows through a crowd or through an individual as a wave of shock, where a set of habits or beliefs clashes with another, or with an event it cannot comprehend or accept.

According to this view, existence is always a dynamic relation between libidinal events, the occurrence of desires in bodies, and economic systems, that is, the structures that allow many different desires to be organized and flow according to pre-set goals and pathways. We need desires as expressions of intensity to keep structures from becoming overly established and fixed. When this occurs they repress other intensities and clash violently with other structures, while at the same time losing their own energy dependent on new flows of intensity.

Thirdly, in Lyotard's philosophy politics is divided between forms of government (this keeps the name politics) and the political (that is, the political and philosophical thought triggered by and true to events). All events, and hence all structures and intensities, can be aspects of the political. But politics is a restricted and impoverished, often negative, form of the political. This split between politics and the political can be traced through all of Lyotard's political writings, from his early activism for the Algerian war of independence and revolution, through his critique of established politics in France in the 1970s and 1980s, up to his ideas about postmodernity and the end of a strong relation between dominant political theories and politics (the end of Marxism as a force in politics, for example).

There are three serious objections to each of the consequences outlined above. First, if we reject ways of relating different discourses or positions, are we not committed to irresolvable differences? If that is the case, must we not accept that differences will have to be resolved by force, since mutual understanding does not seem to be possible?

Secondly, if intensity is to be the arbiter of our relations to things and to life, are we not then committed to the risk of despair when there is no such intensity and to the risk of grievous disagreements over intensity, with no appeal to common understanding? In other words, what happens when the energy generated with events is lacking? What happens when that energy leads to conflicting positions?

Thirdly, is the insistence on the political not too broad, in a sense where everything is political? Yet, also, is it not irrelevant to politics, since what is the point of a political action that does not take account of the requirements of government? Is Lyotard a thinker of the margins, in the bad sense of marginalized, because his idea of the political cannot engage with politics or explain how different political demands are to be ordered and decided upon?

Lyotard's position becomes clearer in the answers to these questions. It is not that we should not care for resolutions of arguments and for the understanding of the views and positions of others; rather, it is that we should also be aware of the limits of such resolutions and of forms of knowledge. We should be aware of the flaws of false resolutions and of systems, such as capitalism, that impose such resolutions (through judgements in terms of profit, for example). We should be aware of the flaws in certain definitions of common reason, where they claim that reason resolves differences, when in fact it hides them and ignores them.

The event is then a form of resistance to what Lyotard calls grand narratives: accounts that bring together different discourses (that he calls language games, after Wittgenstein). It is not possible to give a totalizing account, a meta-narrative, that articulates all possible positions. It is not even possible to provide a logical, rational framework for such resolutions. Yet there are attempts to do so. They violently force differences and events into grids and into forms that do not do justice to them. A philosophy of the event resists this violence and testifies for those who suffer under it.

In his well-known work on the postmodern, *The Postmodern Condition* (1979), Lyotard argues that the postmodern is characterized by a disbelief in grand narratives; we no longer believe in grand unifying theories. This means that the postmodern is a state of fragmentation and heterogeneity, that is, where there are different competing accounts around any event and where these cannot be reconciled.

Two serious misconceptions have to be avoided at this point. First, *The Postmodern Condition* is not central to Lyotard's work. It is an offshoot of work done on justice and Kant during the latter half of the 1970s and leading into the 1980s (for example in the important collections of essays *The Inhuman* and *Postmodern Fables*). Secondly, and resulting from this concern with justice, he is not embracing this postmodern fragmentation, as if we had to accept states of injustice and violent conflict resolution.

On the contrary, Lyotard's poststructuralism asks the question: how can we do justice to the event and bring different sides to accept their differences, rather than adopt one or other false resolution? This is a philosophy based around testimony to events that resist one-sided approaches or complete identification as objects of knowledge. There are limits to knowledge and to procedures of reconciliation. These limits are crucial to any just and sensitive way of responding to events and to the feelings that reveal them.

Even in the quite extreme, but also very beautiful (in the sense of emotionally complex and imaginatively deep and rigorous) *Libidinal Economy* it is not that intensity or energy occur independent of structures that bind them and relate them. Although there are different intensities and events, they are connected through different people through shared structures. Furthermore, structure and forms of knowledge depend on intensity and energy for their evolution and significance.

It is not as if there is a state without intensity and free of the influence of events, and a state of pure intensity with the occurrence of events.

Instead, we have different degrees of intensity and different roles played by events in all structures. The key principle is that no structure fully accounts for the intensities that circulate through it, transform it and bring it to clash with others.

The despair of being left without any emotional drive associated with events is not a certain destiny for Lyotard. Instead, the challenge is how to be as open to events as possible and how to channel their transformative energy through structures as fully as possible. This challenge must chart a path between the desire for pure intensity, which is impossible to fulfil since structures are necessary, and the desire for pure structure and absolute knowledge, which is equally impossible, since structures always conceal the remnants of the intensity of events and openings on to new events. This leads to a response to the third objection. It is not that there is a pure divide between politics and the political; rather, between the two there is a difference in emphasis with respect to events. They inform one another, rather than stand in complete opposition. *The political is primarily a relation to events and to emotional intensities, whereas politics is primarily a reflection on how to achieve goals and on which structures are right and necessary for that achievement.*

Lyotard cannot be committed to an absolute difference between the political and politics, because this would mean that politics was somehow immune to the event. On the contrary, it is that politics must be brought back to the event as something it has drifted away from, necessarily in some sense, but not without remedy. For example, Lyotard is not opposed to human rights, when he discusses them in *The Differend*. Rather, he is concerned about the causes, feelings and events that any particular account of such rights and legal systems excludes (when women were denied the right to vote, for instance). For him, there can be no perfect legal system or account of rights, or even a way to progress towards them on an ever more secure path.

This is because any narrative justifying rights and grounding a legal system must be particular rather than universal; it is written from a point view, in a particular language, rather than from nowhere or everywhere: "In order to judge in this way [against differends], you have therefore neglected the particular stories (diegeses) told by these narratives and singled out the form of narrative, which you declare to be identical in each" (TD: 158).

The form of narrative would be a structure that stood outside other narratives. It would provide a deeper universal truth about all narratives and thereby give rules for relating them and judging which were justified or not, which had legitimate claims for inclusion in a truly universal account. But, according to Lyotard, each account, each position, is driven by feelings and events that are true to it in a way that cannot be abstracted from it and positioned in a universal model.

His poststructuralism is therefore one of radical differences and limits. These are constantly overcome, and overcome in ways that can be judged as relatively good or bad. Lyotard has no difficulty with this relativity and with taking positions in this way. The key problem is how the political action takes its place in relation to totalizing or universalizing accounts. Does it pretend to be universal? Or does it resist such movements?

For Lyotard, there will always be feelings and events that are beyond a relative judgement and that it cannot do justice to. It is crucial to remember this in any relative resolution: to engrave the necessary injustice in any partial solution. His philosophy is concerned with doing justice to events. Beyond any relative resolution, it is therefore to remind us that something has always been hidden and missed.

Politics is about the relative resolutions, but the political is about responding to aesthetic events, to feelings, to matter and to their effects, in such a way as to remind politics of its limits and limitations. This is to allow it to become better, but without falling into the illusion that this process is one that eliminates troublesome events.

Any act is always political and part of politics. This can become hidden in dreams of pure politics (just systems) or dreams of pure political acts (just acts). To guard against this, politics must always be set with aesthetic events and with creative political acts that destroy false universality and dreams of perfect understanding and resolutions.

To sense the power of this claim more fully, it is important to focus on Lyotard's precise arguments against universal structures, and his arguments against references to facts or to objectivity. It is not that he gives us a particular position that may be interesting from a political point of view; rather, it is that he has developed a thorough critique of possible appeals to a ground for truthful statements based on structure or facts. To follow these arguments in the context of poststructuralism, it is important to turn to his most academic and carefully argued book, *Discours, figure*.

Poststructuralism and the figural

Discours, figure puts Lyotard's views on aesthetic events and structures into practice as an explicit reaction to structuralism. The book contains a series of figures and artworks that are meant to work as events that disrupt discourse, as well as fixed relations of sense and reference. The book is therefore designed to be a theoretical study and an aesthetic event. Once again, this is the performative and practical aspect of post-structuralism: it enacts, rather than merely says, argues, or dictates. *Discours, figure* is more than a theoretical work; it has intricate aesthetic qualities of its own, in particular, in the relation between text and illustrations. In fact, "illustration" is the wrong word, since the paintings and figures in the book are meant to transform our reception of the text, rather than simply provide cases or examples.

Lyotard coins the term "figural" to describe the association of matter and feeling in the aesthetic event. For example, a painting is figural in the way it always goes beyond descriptions of it and theories about it. It is neither an objective figure or shape, nor a figure in a language: it is a process between the two. The painting or artwork is also figural in always adding to and transforming what it depicts or refers to. This is achieved through feelings allied to the matter of the figure. The figural is this association of their intensity with the openness and ambiguity of matter. The work in not a closed figure, but an open matter associated with feelings.

The following passages are some of the most important from *Discours, figure*. They explain how language (signification) and things (designation) cannot account for sense. In this passage, sense is not simply meaning, but individual intensity, or the reason why any given meaning matters or is intense for us:

> Signification does not exhaust sense, but neither does the conjunction of signification and designation. Discourse slips from one alternative space to the other, between the space of the system and the space of the subject. We must not remain stuck with them. (DF: 135)

The failure of the space of language, and the failure of the space of the things that we can refer to, must be understood as a failure to account for the extra emotional intensity that occurs with events. It demands a further space to explain how language and things evolve and how they acquire a special, changeable and dynamic meaning for us.

This space is defined as the figural. It is neither objective, nor subjective. Instead, it brings both together by transforming and challenging them.

> There is another space – the figural. We have to see it as concealed, it does not reveal itself to sight, nor to thought. It is

> indicated laterally, a fugitive within discourses and perceptions, as that which troubles them. It is the space proper to desire – the stake of the struggle that painters and poets pursue ceaselessly against the return of the Ego and the text. (DF: 135)

The need to approach the figural laterally is due to the limits of significance or of knowledge. It is also due to the limitations of reference or of appeals to brute things and to nature. If the figural could be approached in these ways, then it would collapse on to one or the other; there would either be full knowledge of the figural, or a capacity to refer to it or to point to it in objects.

Lyotard's interest in art and aesthetics comes from this need to go beyond knowledge and to invoke feelings that cannot be captured or identified. This is why he resists the "Ego" in the sense of a well-determined meaning and understanding that we could grasp within us. It is also why he resists the notion of a fixed meaning defined within given texts. Instead, desire is always something that works outside these certainties. Yet desire sets them in motion and gives them direction.

Key poststructuralist challenges arise in Lyotard's work with more force than elsewhere: what are meaning and understanding without desire? What is life without desire and without the unpredictable changes that desire brings to life? Why is desire only approached well through art and creativity? How can we do justice to the special realm of desires and to the role it plays secretly within knowledge and the world?

As a figural event, a painting is a process that creates and destroys discourse and referents. It destroys knowledge and objective reality. Painting unleashes feelings and desires into systems that live off them, but that also resist them. However, this release has a wider point. Lyotard is not only concerned with the diminution of intensity in structures. He is concerned to encourage the formation of new structures and to show how some structures come to dominate our ways of thinking in illegitimate ways.

In *Discours, figure*, Lyotard is interested in aesthetic events that mark the transition between forms of discourse that are opposed to one another. He charts their different views of reality and referents, then shows how they can be connected through the desires they repress and channel. The world changes with the discourses about it, but the reason both change is not internal to the world or to discourse. It is driven by the power of the figural event and its role between the two of them.

So Lyotard's poststructuralism seeks to explain the changes, evolutions and revolutions of discourses as well as their relation to what they refer to. It does so by appealing to a special matter, the figural, and to figural events where feelings flow through language and reality.

For example, in *Discours, figure* Lyotard follows the shift in art and in our understanding of the world when perspective is introduced into painting in Italy in the fifteenth century. He explains the shift through the event of a different way of feeling towards paintings as they acquire depth. Before perspective, paintings are supposed to work as signs to be read; after, they are supposed to work as windows on the world.

The shift in painting is therefore meant to accompany a shift from a discourse on the world based on signs and reading, to a discourse based on a spatial nature: to be moved through and experienced. But Lyotard does not accept these hypotheses. In typical poststructuralist fashion, he reflects on this apparently obvious divide and sees connections and extensions, where others see fixed oppositions.

Before perspective there is still a sense of motion, and afterwards there is still a sense of reading. In both, the world is something to be experienced and something to be read. When either theory gains ascendancy, something is missed about the nature of the world and about our discourse upon it. Lyotard also shows this in *Discours, figure* through a highly detailed and rigorous study of the role of illustration in medieval religious texts. There is not only the word, but also figure and colour allied to the word, so the texts are sensual experiences as well as sensual ones.

The figural in painting shows that there is something more than what a discourse can say about it, more than what any discourse can say about it. It also shows there is something more to matter than either the view that it is something that works like a text or something like objects in a space to be moved through and experienced. The figural is therefore opposed to any final theory about the form of knowledge (discourse) and its referent (reality, the world).

Lyotard's poststructuralism therefore appeals to the figural as a means to be sceptical about knowledge and about an independent reality. This does not mean that poststructuralism is anti-knowledge or completely opposed to practical appeals to an independent reality. Rather, it means that it insists that their claims have important limits and that they cannot be understood fully without reference to events that resist established forms of knowledge or views of reality.

Any given discourse that denies its own origin, in feeling and in a matter that it cannot fully grasp, fails to understand its own value. It over-inflates its claims to truth. Instead of thinking that there is a move to greater truth when we shift from a representation of the world as a flat surface to one in terms of perspective, Lyotard claims that the truth is in the events that drive this change, not in the two starting-points:

> A discourse [in this case, science] that excludes the presence of the figural from itself, cannot cross what separates it from its object – it forbids itself from becoming expressive. The window traced by Masaccio on the wall does not give on to the discovery of a world, but of its loss, one could say that it is its discovery as lost. The window is not open and, in allowing us to see, the pane of representation separates. It makes that space oscillate over there, not here (as in a *trompe l'oeil*), nor elsewhere, as in Duccio. (DF: 201)

This passage on painting and discourse is important because it shows Lyotard's refusal to accept that we are presented with the following alternative: either discourse and knowledge can satisfactorily represent their object and there is a perfect fit between the two, or the two have no correspondence whatsoever and knowledge fails to rejoin the object. This failure then leads to radical scepticism and despair: the opposite to the misplaced confidence of the position it negates. Instead, Lyotard insists on an oscillation and a connection that can never finally turn into a perfect representation. He redefines the true relation of discourse to its object as an expressive one, that is, as one that demands an aesthetic form. We have to create discourse in such a way as it continues to move with its object and to evolve with it that neither comes to a halt in an identification.

Expression depends on events that trigger the creative process. The events protect the process from the dream of a perfect capture of its object, either through a perfect representation (a space that oscillates here), or through an appeal to an external guarantee of perfection (a space that oscillates elsewhere). Lyotard's poststructuralism is therefore not an appeal to art as a privileged realm separate from all others. It is an appeal to heed the lesson of a particular experience of art involving a sensual and destabilizing experience of matter. This experience allows us to feel that we misunderstand reality and knowledge when we separate them from a very precise sensual experience.

In poststructuralism, this experience is not the mystical transmission of an other-worldly message. Lyotard is always opposed to this return to a higher mystical discourse. Neither is the experience a direct encounter with matter, finally grasped in all its truth. The view that the brute facts of existence could be grasped is a terrible misunderstanding of the complexity and mobility of feelings and desires in relation to matter.

Art and the figural allow us to experience a productive gap between our understanding and matter. They do this through our senses, no longer defined as strict functions relating us to the qualities of objects, but as disruptive mediators between changing discourses and fluid matter.

Truth and poststructuralism

Of the thinkers covered in this book, Lyotard invites certain important criticisms that apply to all poststructuralists most directly and with greatest force. This is because his dependence on feelings to undermine meaning and reference seems to be a straightforward case of denying traditional ways to agreement and to knowledge, but on the most subjective and individual basis. We are driven to ask how a philosopher can deny that truth must depend upon common ideas about the validity of arguments and the truth of statements about the world or objects in the world. Where would we stand without such truths and validity, if not in a brutal world of appeals to force or to mystical inspiration?

Indeed, in his refusal to define feelings in terms of empirical science, or by giving them an easily graspable identity, Lyotard seems to be siding with unreason and passion in such an extreme way that accusations of relativism and irresponsibility are hard to avoid. However, the issues are far more complicated than they seem. If we look at the following passages on truth from *Discours, figure*, we see that his position is much more nuanced than simple caricatures might lead us to believe:

> But truth happens (e-venit) as that which is not where it should be; it is essentially displaced; as such, promised to elision: no place for it, not foreseen, nor foreknown. On the contrary, everything is in place in the spaces of signification and designation so that its effects appear as simple errors, slip-ups due to inattention, to the misalignment of pieces of discourse, to the poor adaptation of the eye. Everything is in place for the effacement of the event – for the restoration of good form, of clear and distinct thought. Truth is presented as a fall, slippage, error: the meaning of the Latin *lapsus*. The event opens a space and time of vertigo, it is not tied to its context or perceptual environment. This discontinuity or floating is paired with anxiety. (DF: 135)

Truth is an event in the strong sense of something that happens in an unpredictable and troubling manner. It cannot be known or grasped, only felt and expressed. Traditional ways of identifying things as true cannot take account of such events except by defining them as errors. This is because (after Descartes) they seek clear and distinct identifications of things, whereas events are blurred and moving encounters of feelings and matter.

Lyotard is not claiming that there is only the truth of the event, or that it can stand independently of other truths. Rather, he is claiming that the truth of the event is something hidden and expelled by other ideas of truth ("promised to elision"). His point is not that we should simply deny reference or validity. It is that there is something else that also matters.

Furthermore, as in other poststructuralists, the reason this other truth matters is due to its capacity to allow us to think in more open and flexible ways: "it is not tied to its context or perceptual environment". Feelings are therefore necessary to jolt us out of a position of complacency, for example, when we are incapable of seeing that strangers have an important point to make, until we sense the desperation to communicate their side of a story or conflict.

The reason this truth has to be presented through feelings that defy definition is that established structures of knowledge and forms of reference through identification cannot allow for radically new events. This is due to the way they prejudge what form those events must fit. Because they resist identification as objects of knowledge, events have to be seen as "errors" or cases of "misalignment" or "poor adaptation".

This explains Lyotard's appeal to the feeling of vertigo. The event must make us dizzy. This disorientation leads us to question our relation to well-ordered space and time. The vertigo indicates a failure of that order in terms of our feelings towards it. We can then either say that this failure is a weakness of our feelings, a failure of the event, and can then see them as something to be avoided and to be expelled as false (or as a *lapsus*) or, with Lyotard, we can see the feeling and event as revealing a deeper truth about the world. The arguments are finely balanced here, since order allows us to achieve aims in a practical and apparently common way. Truths associated with knowledge and with order are crucial to our well-being and to social cohesion. Lyotard does not deny this. However, such truths are not all there is and, from his point of view, great damage can be done if this is not acknowledged.

Lyotard's poststructuralism is a plea for an extension of truth, rather than a plea for the denial of truths that have long been useful to us and helpful in social and moral interactions. For him, we have to understand how knowledge comes to change, what its limits are, and what we eliminate or lose when we forget these limits. It is a matter of a receptivity to feelings that indicate exclusion or radical differences.

This is why he speaks of discontinuity when he addresses the truth of vertigo or of the event. The event shows that there are discontinuities between different claims to truth and between truth based on consistency and identity, and truth responding to events. This discontinuity does not mean we can avoid consistent systems and claims to identity; they are conditions for discontinuity.

Theory and practice

A further key aspect of poststructuralism, shown well in Lyotard's work, is the denial of the theory and practice distinction. Poststructuralists do not believe that theory can be separate from practice. More radically, they believe that theory is practice, not in the sense of a practice among many, but in the sense of a practical and ongoing experimentation with matter. So theories are not applied to practical situations; they emerge in them and cannot stand independently of them. This explains why all of Lyotard's books and essays are practical, in the sense of experimental work on a case or within a matter. They do not present a theory, only then to apply it or test it later. Instead, theoretical terms come out of and can only be explained in practical cases.

This has two important effects that must not be overlooked when studying his work. First, the style of his works is experimental because it is an attempt to approach his material free of any appeal to a completely external and neutral vocabulary. He has to make us feel for his points and material, as if we are part of both. His main terms cannot be free of experiment and variation in terms of the material. Secondly, his works always address something outside any pre-set theoretical frame and do so by attempting to add something to them, in the sense of becoming part of the works and cases. So when Lyotard writes on painters (as he does often and very beautifully) he is not judging or categorizing the works. He is trying to create with them: to make them live for us in stronger and different ways.

This explains why Lyotard's style varies so much through his work, since he adapts it to suit the material and the feelings he wants to communicate. He has used shock, humour, irony, sensibility, ellipsis, dialogue, fragments, aphorisms and careful scholarly exposition at different times. Each attempt is carefully crafted to unite philosophical reflection and material. It is therefore important to read Lyotard with an ear for his style and what it is trying to do. For example, his ironic and humorous essays in *The Inhuman* and *Postmodern Fables* can be read as straight academic theses. But such readings miss the important points that Lyotard is making. Ideas come up against events that show them to be false abstractions.

This showing works through the humorous and ironic turn taken by abstract ideas when they are extended to absurd limits or placed unyieldingly in practical situations. So when he describes the idea of a post-human future he is not simply advocating this idea but rather trying to get us to think and feel what that idea implies and presupposes.

Poststructuralism is more engaged with its material, and in richer ways, than simple structuralism and many other theoretical and abstract forms of thought. This has the advantage of making poststructuralist texts much better at bringing out what is of value, what is living, in that material. But it also means that the risks of tendentious and divisive readings increases on both sides, for example, when Lyotard's irony around universal values is read straight or when poststructuralist works simply ignore knowledge about a certain material.

This resistance to theoretical abstraction also makes poststructuralism well suited to interdisciplinary work. This is because barriers between subjects are overcome through the material they share. Instead of having, say, art-historical and philosophical theories about art, we have different and connected interactions with a similar material. In turn, this explains Lyotard's influence in subjects outside philosophy. His work is a prompt to thought and a powerful reservoir of ideas, rather than an attempt to give a last word on material; thereby, it avoids conflicts between "last words" on something. It also avoids the divisive misunderstandings between theories across disciplines, where one judges the other not on what it is trying to do, but on what it explicitly is not trying to do.

There can be a portentousness and high seriousness to philosophy and to academic debate. It has the value of holding truths dear and of seeking clear moral and political guidance. Against this value of certainty, poststructuralism asks us to give a little on fixed truths and theories, so that we can be more truthful to individual cases and to the events that occur with them. This explains why Lyotard's texts on many different artists are not yet as well known as their depth and sensitivity deserves. When he writes on Monory, Duchamp, Baruchello, Newman, Francken, Adami, Arakawa and Buren he writes with the artists rather than about them. This leads to fragile and sensitive assemblies of thoughts, styles and artworks. But it does not lead to a "theory of art" that can accompany final judgements about good and bad art, or high and low art. It is easier and more prevalent to think in terms of these categories, but Lyotard's approach does greater justice to the works and to their deep and individual value.

In his poststructuralism, the questions "What is this?", "Where does it belong?", "What does it mean?" and "Is it good?" are replaced by the questions "Did it work for you?", "How did it work for you?", "What can be done with this?" and "What is of value here, for you, now?". It is easy to attack this shift in questions as a move to irresponsibility, since it appears to encourage a sense of equality between works. Yet this is completely wrong in two important ways.

First, it is not the case that any commentary goes with respect to the works. On the contrary, the challenge is to bring out what they can teach us and allow us to do. This challenge involves deeply felt selections and rejections alongside historical and contemporary structures of truth and knowledge. It is a careful, intricate and selective work, rather than sweeping generalization or declamation. Ironically, this kind of thought is the most common one deployed against poststructuralist works. This critique is often an ill-informed argument and lazy response to the difficulty and precision of poststructuralism, rather than to its relativism.

Secondly, the attitude to the works is more "truthful" and "moral" with Lyotard, since, instead of standing outside them and treating them in terms of independent categories and ideas, he works with them and tries to bring out their intrinsic values. In this sense, the empirical aspect of poststructuralism is present in Lyotard's work on art. It is an attempt to give full voice to works through experimentation.

Once again, here, the meaning of empirical is a special one. This is because, in avoiding the distinction between theory and practice, Lyotard also goes beyond notions of empirical tests of separate theories (either in terms of confirmation or refutation). For him, the theory emerges with the material and with the event. It is not so much tested as "evolved with". The experiment is about creating new theory–matter relations true to events, rather than theories about things that are not altered by them. Theory and material make one another, rather than determine one another as truthful and as known.

The relation is therefore more like the one of parent to child, where both learn and evolve together; rather than one applying a distinct theory to the other and the other providing facts for gauging the success and failure of theories. This does not mean that there are not theories. There are, and they are tested in the usual way, but each parent–child relation is something more than that: it is a mutual learning in the light of theories and beyond them towards what is singular in each loving relationship.

Therefore, in *Discours, figure*, Lyotard does not define the figural in abstraction from works. Instead, he multiplies varieties of the figural to account for the different functions of disturbance found in different works. Here is his description of the deconstructive power of a Picasso drawing:

> We have an illustration of [the transgression of a revealing trace] in this drawing by Picasso [nude study 1941] where the object of the deconstruction is the edge, the line that marks a single unifying and reifying point of view. The coexistence of many contours induces a simultaneity of many points of view. The scene where this woman sleeps does not belong to the "real" space, since it tolerates many positions for a body in a same time and space. Erotic indifference to time and to reality in favour of postures. (DF: 277)

In terms of understanding the power of desire created by figures, Picasso shows us how figures work in a different form of time and space than the one we ordinarily associate with reality. Desire is a relation to many postures in one space. We literally experience that multiplicity in Picasso's drawing and in other relations to desired flesh and postures.

The Picasso drawing is an event that undermines the notion that all things have clearly defined spatial and temporal limits. Traces, in the sense of boundaries, do not reveal the proper limits of an object. They can be made to reveal many incommensurable limits in one place. For Lyotard, desire and sensations are driven by such events. These are experiences where reality is opened up and shown to be much more than what is defined by a given discourse, understanding or reference.

In response to the question "How can reality and knowledge keep giving rise to new desires?", Lyotard answers that desire feeds into "reality" and "knowledge". It continuously renews them and shows them to be flexible and open, where we could think of them as closed and fixed. This power of desire as event is traced through his work, as that which allows life to survive boredom, despair and nihilism (and the desperate violence that they engender, often in hidden ways and where it is not expected).

Desire and reality: the poststructural city

Poststructuralism opens up the world and allows multiple views to replace a single homogeneous one. This is not done at the expense of senses of life as well ordered, but in order to provide a foil to that order. Throughout *Discours, figure*, Lyotard shifts from necessary illusions of order to new releases of desire associated with new feelings and perceptions of matter. These new events are ways of experiencing reality as different and multiple; they call for new discourses and for the creation of further new events.

In his description of a move that adds to the restricted Cartesian spatiotemporal account of the city (in terms of a rectangular grid), he argues that any rational frame is always related to experiences and to views that it excludes. Reason is always related to its other. He shows this move at work even in the description of the city in Descartes's *Discourse on Method*.

Descartes's work has to keep a grid account together with an account that begins from a seeing subject (and that is therefore curved). We have to work with a map that imposes a rectangular and uniform grid on the city, yet each time we project ourselves into the map or look back out on to the city it curves away and fragments into a jumble of scales according to our lines of vision and horizons. According to Lyotard, this multiplicity of views creates a tension that cannot be resolved. However, Cartesian rationalism and its legacy view the tension as a negative, to be overcome as best we can in practice and totally in theory, whereas Lyotard's poststructuralism adopts it as a positive site of productive differences to be fed into each view.

There is therefore not one city, but many:

> The destiny that ensures that *ratio* is born from its other takes its model from the world of culture. It is like a town whose visible configuration of streets and districts contains another configuration, the one it gave a century ago, and another again. Each is linked to the others through urban planning, sometimes visible, sometimes hidden, such that when the mind strolls through the town it experiences a fundamental mobility.   (DF: 183–4)

So the city is layered through the signs of its history and no layer can claim to be free of the others. The key words here are "experience" and "fundamental mobility". Lyotard claims that different experiences of the city cannot be closed off and that genuine experience – the experience of a figural event – is not of a single city, but of the interrelation of many cities.

No single view of the city can claim priority in terms of this interrelation. No single view can claim to return us to some final legitimate sense of order. Instead, the experience is always one of shifting relations with no external ordering principle: "This is not only its displacement with respect to a plan of the city that one could assume fixed and self-identical. It is the simultaneous displacement of the parts of the plan" (DF: 184).

Not only are there many cities in one, but each part of the city is itself multiple: "That means that, in passing from one district to another, and, at the limit, in looking at a same monument, at an apparently homogeneous building, the mind passes from one city to another, from one moment of the self to another" (DF: 184). There is a radical fragmentation of the city, in this move from unity to moments of experience. Each part is fragmented according to the different views around it and according to their disruptive interrelation.

A sign of this heterogeneity and of this multiplication of views can be found in the different challenges put to city planners. The debate about a new building or plan is never a homogeneous discussion; instead, different emotional, historical, economic and political views clash in terms of what they value and what they dream of creating and preserving. They literally bring different cities to the table.

Lyotard's view is not that these positions cannot work together. They have to. Instead, what is a stake is how they work together: towards an illusory single view or towards an enrichment of the city's capacity to generate different ones. Are the debates respectful of an original series of differences and of their creative openness? Or is this multiplicity reduced and denied? What structures are put in place to preserve one or deny the other? How can these structures be challenged and opened up?

Lyotard argues that the city's fragmentation resists a satisfactory reunification, because the moments are not present in each other's vision in the same way. They are transformed each time: "Each of these moments orders the others around itself and appears as a focus around which all the other moments (the other places of the city) are deformed, bent, unrecognisable" (DF: 184). This is the key to the resistance to a totalizing reductive view, since each one transforms the other, so there is never a shared representation, even of each position for the other.

At the planning meeting, it is not that different citizens refuse to understand one another. It is that they see different things and the things they see differently include each others' claims. Again, that the best structure to resolve these differences lies in democracy, understanding and mutual respect is not denied in Lyotard's work. Rather, he wants to remind us of the reasons why these good tools may still fail us, how they cannot escape corruption, and how they need constant challenges and renewals. Failure in the face of events is valuable through the lessons it teaches us for more careful reconstruction.

But there is no overarching reason for the guidance of this reconstruction: "rationality, from a 'good' point of view, will only be able to construct itself at the price of neglecting, in principle, this peripheral curvature, this childhood, this event" (DF: 184). The crisis caused by events and by feelings invites us to think differently, rather than to seek a reason free of crises: "The crisis in the world of the mind, the crisis of culture, returns us, through the metaphor of the city, to the crisis caused in the understanding by the world of vision – a crisis of passion" (DF: 184).

The question then becomes: how can we respond to the necessary neglect implied by the dominance of one point of view? The answer is by paying heed to the event, to our feelings towards it, to the limits that it shows within established structures, to their capacity for neglect, but also to their capacity for responding to the event. It is a call for a careful and attentive creativity, rather than for a blind and ruthless revolution.

It is tempting to react to fragmentation in a negative way, accusing it of relativism and senseless division. How can different experiences be related at all? Are some not more truthful than others? How can we define or grasp any experience, since it can itself be subdivided?

From the argument of *Discours, figure*, these questions stand on a mistaken premise. It is not that we have either order or chaos, unity or intractable difference, certainty or complete absence of any norms or values. Instead, structures provide relative order, certainty, norms and values. These are related to a constituted reality or referent. But structures are not all there is. Instead, there are wider experiences (events) that are essential in explaining the significance of the structures, their capacity to change and their limits: "the gap between sign and word will never be crossed" (DF: 185).

Poststructuralist political action: testifying to the differend

But what happens when Lyotard's views on structure and the event are put into practice in pragmatic political situations? Can his suspicion of foundational structures and fixed truths and his belief in the truth of the event lead into effective political action? Or does it lead to prevarication and despair, or to senseless and disjointed political action? Does a poststructuralist philosophy of the event lead to a new individualism, or can it be the basis of genuinely effective action for better communities? An answer to these questions can be found in the closing sections of *The Differend*, where he argues for action against the background of the despair and lack of direction that comes from disbelief in grand narratives. These closing aphorisms then link into his books on politics and aesthetics after Kant (*L'Enthousiasme* and *Lessons on the Analytic of the Sublime*).

In *The Differend*, Lyotard sets out the idea of the end of grand narratives in terms of Kant's search for guiding threads in politics and history. These guiding threads are ideas that bring together different historical and political situations by setting them within a wider account, for example, under the idea of progress through political freedom and rational science.

Sublime events are supposed to confirm these guiding threads, against the inevitable confusion and apparent lack of direction of history. We believe in the benefits of the Enlightenment, when we experience a sublime feeling of enthusiasm after witnessing an event that confirms such an idea ("Yes. People can be guided by a rational idea to rise up and seek a better world.") It is important to distinguish between witnessing or being a spectator and being involved in the event. For the latter, the sublime feeling cannot confirm the idea, because those involved are too close to the action.

However, according to Lyotard history has provided cases that stand as the exact opposite to sublime events confirming progressive ideas or what he calls signs of history. Names of twentieth-century events (Auschwitz, Berlin 1953, Budapest 1956, Czechoslovakia 1968, Poland 1980) stand as counters to any positive events we can think of, for example, around the liberations at the end of the Second World War, or at the fall of the Berlin Wall (which occurred after publication of *The Differend*). The power of the guiding thread is negated and we are left in a situation of despair with regard to thoughts of political progress and human emancipation: "The passages promised by the great doctrinal syntheses end in bloody impasses. Whence the sorrow of the spectators in this end of the twentieth century" (TD: 180). We do not pass to ever-higher better stages, but remain mired in cycles of hope punctuated by death and destruction.

This argument appears to put Lyotard in a very difficult position, since, by this stage of his book, he has portrayed capitalism as a way of articulating other forms of language that destroys their capacity to resist it. He has also turned against appeals to communal identities in the struggle to resist capitalism: "The resistance of communities banded around their names and their narratives is counted on to stand in the way of capital's hegemony. This is a mistake" (TD: 181). It is a mistake from the point of view of Lyotard's double critique of narrative. On the one hand, narratives are always narratives of inclusions and exclusions, insiders and outsiders, the chosen and the damned. There is no narrative that speaks for everyone and, when we tell "our" story, it is always restricted. On the other hand, narrative feeds into capitalism, providing it with material to circulate and to ascribe value to. A narrative is a way of turning an event into a commodity. It transforms the event into a form that can be exchanged with others, rendering the singular accessible to wider forms of understanding and hence valuation.

So narratives break down resistance, even if it is in the name of a universal, because they contradict the universal claims through the necessary parochialism of the narrative. They also fail to halt the ever-accelerating circulation of capital. Lyotard's comment on this is wistful and reminds us of his work on Algeria and its independence, but lack of revolution: "Proud struggles for independence end in young, reactionary States" (TD: 181). But this does not mean that Lyotard abandons resistance, or that his version of resistance becomes all the more desperate and violent. Instead, he stresses the ambiguous role of capital as liberating and enslaving: as seeking out productive differences but then reducing them to sameness. He also seeks a form of resistance that cannot be recuperated in the same way as narrative.

Within this ambiguity and against this power of recuperation there is still a possibility for resistance: "The only insurmountable obstacle that the hegemony of the economic genre comes up against is the heterogeneity of phrase regimens and of genres of discourse" (TD: 181). This means that, for Lyotard, resistance lies in insisting that certain things cannot be given a value that equates them to others. These things are the condition for incommensurability between ways of understanding the world, reflecting on the good, or making judgements of value.

It does not mean that understanding, reason and judgement have no value, or that they should be opposed. Rather, it means that there is an additional condition for their role within resistance. They must be supplemented by an awareness of what they have not understood, reasoned through or judged: "The obstacle does not depend upon the 'will' of human beings in one sense or in another, but upon the differend. The differend is reborn from the very resolution of supposed litigations" (TD: 181). So, when we seek to resolve injustices and work for the good, we should also work to bear witness to what remains beyond resolution.

There are two practical ways of doing this. First, all solutions must be criticized and undermined in their claims to perfection and final truths. Their temporary and fragile nature should be shown through a critique of universalizing and totalizing vocabulary, and through a critique of statements regarding final ends. We can never have done with differences. We can never arrive at a perfect end. Although we should continue to seek to resist, not for an end, or for a certain progress, but because the differences demand it:

> [The differend] summons humans to situate themselves in unknown phrase universes, even if they don't have the feeling that something has to be phrased. (For this is a necessity and not an obligation.) The *Is it happening?* is invincible to every will to gain time. (TD: 181)

The "*Is it happening?*" is the sublime event that makes us feel that there is a difference beyond resolution. The will to gain time is the essence of capitalism: to reduce differences so that they may circulate more efficiently.

Secondly, we should testify to these differences in positive ways. Not by criticizing the failures of the structures we have to work through in order to resist effectively, but by giving voice to events creatively. Lyotard calls us to create events as much as to respond to them. Events do not happen to us because we are passive, in the sense of transfixed spectators, but because we are always experimenting with ways to open ourselves up to the unexpected, to the foreign and to that which we have excluded.

By seeking to be what you are not, you make it possible for others to exist as different. But this can have no guarantees, or paths to success. It is a calling and not a rational plan: "You can't make a political 'program' with it, but you can bear witness to it" (TD: 181).

five

Poststructuralism, history, genealogy: Michel Foucault's *The Archaeology of Knowledge*

Poststructuralism and history

Michel Foucault's poststructuralism is developed through a series of historical studies. His work is remarkable in seeking to change the way history is written, while resisting a straightforward move to structuralist methods. He is therefore more of a philosopher-historian than simply one or the other. Foucault will not be presented here simply as a historian; this would restrict the significance of his thought within wider ideas of poststructuralism. However, a reading of the importance of his thought for history and for philosophy will be one of the main lines of enquiry.

Mid-career, Foucault reflected on his new philosophy of history in relation to structuralism in the influential book *The Archaeology of Knowledge* (1969). The book is key to understanding Foucault's relation to structuralism, a relation that includes common themes as well as divergences in terms of methods and philosophical presuppositions. It comes between Foucault's early works *Madness and Civilisation* (1961), *Birth of the Clinic* (1963) and *The Order of Things* (1966) and his later works *Discipline and Punish* (1975) and the three volumes of *The History of Sexuality* (1976, 1984, 1984). Foucault published many more works around these main books; these are often brought together in influential collections such as *Power/Knowledge* (1980).

This chapter will follow through his arguments by drawing out three key aspects:

- Foucault's new philosophy of history;

- the outlines of a poststructuralist way of writing history and acting upon it in the present;
- the contrasts between this philosophy and way of writing and structuralist methods.

These aspects capture the extent of Foucault's influence on poststructuralist philosophy. He provides new ways of thinking about our relation to the past. He gives us complex and powerful methods for writing history. His work is a revolutionary departure from what came before, not only in terms of history, but in terms of philosophies of time and of social conditioning. In short, Foucault provides us with a new, poststructuralist, form of historical critique.

The relation between social structures and individuals is looked at in a different way in Foucault's work. This transforms our understanding of those structures. This is one side of his poststructuralism. The work also transforms our ideas about what an individual is, in particular, in terms of freedom and power. This is its other side. There is a relentless critical approach to the free subject and to the central role of free will in his work. Power is no longer associated with free actors, but with new ideas about structures, language and time.

After Foucault, life must be seen as an engagement with long and tangled historical genealogies. We cannot escape the evolving forms that make us, our spaces and our times. Action can only take place within these forms. It must be free of the illusion that there can be a final truth to the genealogy. It must avoid the ideas that the complexity of genealogies can either be reduced to simple causal lines or be free of contingency.

Foucault stresses historical conditioning, contingency and openness. This means that his work can neither be associated with crude versions of Marxism, since he does not believe in historical determinism, nor lined up with liberalism, since he does not believe in free human subjects. Like many poststructuralists, his work falls between determinism and freedom. We are historically conditioned, but take our place in an open and contingent system.

This position between necessity and freedom is problematic on many fronts. The following contradictions and problems draw out serious challenges to Foucault's works. These challenges are persistent counters to his thought:

- How can an act be both free and determined? Either history shows us that the world follows a necessary path or it shows us that it is driven by free acts. It makes no sense to insist on the role of genealogy but also to insist on the openness of the future.

- How can history be defined as irreducibly complex without pre-judging the possibility of finding a logic to it? Is not any effort to understand history an effort to reduce that complexity and to find the continuities that underlie apparently chance-driven processes?
- Should there not be a science of history, if we speak of determinism or genealogy? If we are determined or genealogically conditioned, it must be according to scientific causal laws; therefore, it makes no sense to speak of the openness of the future, since the sciences will demonstrate the laws we have to work under.
- If we speak of freedom, it must be in terms of the freedom of human subjects to act in one way or another. History should therefore be about the relation of human subjects to the ideas and to the facts that they can consider prior to action. It therefore makes no sense to write a history of genealogies, unless this is subservient to the role of human freedom and to scientific objectivity.

The Archaeology of Knowledge is one of Foucault's main attempts to answer these questions (and many others) in response to the reception of his earlier histories. In the first part of the book he defines what is new about history in his time. Towards the end of the chapter it becomes clear that he is speaking about his work and about its critical context.

In an imaginary dialogue, setting the new historian against detractors complaining about apparent changes in his position, Foucault gives the following answer, which captures many of the key facets of his thought:

> What, do you imagine that I would take so much trouble and so much pleasure in writing, do you think that I would keep so persistently to my task, if I were not preparing – with a rather shaky hand – a labyrinth into which I can venture, in which I can move my discourse, opening up underground passages, forcing it to go far from itself, finding overhangs that reduce and deform its itinerary, in which I can lose myself and appear at last to eyes that I will never have to meet again. I am no doubt not the only one who writes in order to have no face. Do not ask me to remain the same: leave it to the bureaucrats and our police to see that our papers are in order. At least spare us their morality when we write. (AK: 19)

This passage gives us clues to resolve two important puzzles: first, how to read Foucault or, at least, some principles for not reading him badly, that is, for not reading him fruitlessly and for not learning from him; and secondly, what motivates him. The passage reminds us of his key motivations as developed through his books in different formats and guises. These impulses call for new ways of thinking about power and freedom. They lead to a new way of thinking about the human subject and the writer of history.

The first point to note about Foucault's style, and about principles for reading him, is how quotable he is. Unlike many poststructuralist thinkers, he writes in a very clear and striking manner. He avoids obtuse theoretical terms and each clause in his sentences is accessible. It is easy to find passages to give straightforward evidence for different positions on a wide range of issues. However, this ease of quotation is a trap. Foucault achieves depth and subtlety through variations over series of statements and sentences, rather than through the density of any given sentence or terminology. Reading him is closer to participating in a debate, where positions are clarified over time, and where each statement is only a temporary and alterable part of a series of interlocked contributions.

This means that Foucault must be read with reserve, that is, without jumping to conclusions and with an ear for the variations that take place through his texts. Each subsection of his writing must be read for its clear statement. But, equally, this temporary clarity must be accompanied by care taken towards what is deferred or still in question. Signs for this can be found in the apparent contradictions and crudeness of given sections. These flaws are remedied later. A position that could be viewed as too simple is often extremely complex when viewed in a wider setting. Indeed, it may be overly complex and too open for many tastes.

Foucault ends the first part of *The Archaeology of Knowledge* with a mock dialogue, rather than a straight statement, to allow him to give a simple position, but also to set that view in a broader and more complicated train of thought. The simple position is: "My work is meant to evolve, because I believe in the value of an open creativity that resists identification in terms of meaning and authorship". But he then stops that position from becoming the quotable final word, by reporting it as part of a dialogue. This is the opening on to wider and more difficult strands of thought.

The dialogue projects outwards, undermining any simple interpretation of it as a standalone position. The reader has to see it in context because it differs from that whole in style. It appears as a simplification or exemplification of a wider section. Moreover, the dialogue does not add much of substance to what precedes it. Instead, it varies it slightly, by answering a particular objection: "Why is it so hard to pin you down?" It also answers a particular accusation: "It is morally and epistemologically wrong to avoid identification". In other words, morality relies on a trustworthy identity and knowledge depends on the identity of key ideas through time.

The simple answers to this objection and accusation are that Foucault is so hard to pin down because he believes that the search for self-identity – either in oneself or others – is a bad thing. This is because he values transformation and mobility due to the way they allow us to move outside restrictive structures. It is not that we can escape moral and legal frameworks and their demands for identity; it is that writing and thought should not replicate them, but question them and force them to open up.

It is, therefore, not wrong to avoid identification, but wrong to seek to reinforce it. This is because the nature of the relation of the self and of the subject to structure is not one of perfect fit. On the contrary, the writer – Foucault – is always moving beyond where we expect him to be, or want him to be. This movement is a source of pleasure: a key life-affirming term for Foucault. Do not seek to know who you are, but work with and vary your pleasures and their necessary relation to structures inherited from history.

Pleasure lies in involvement in wider relations of transformation and overcoming. Power lies in structures, in their capacity to determine identities and acts, values and norms. Pleasure is a transgression of power, in that it accompanies a change in structural relations and hence finds space for movement within the inherited determinations of power. Power is the net of historical determinations that we have to struggle in and cannot escape, at least not fully. The passage quoted above is a way into Foucault's original way of thinking about power and about resistance. Power is not in the relation between Foucault and some unnamed questioner. It is the intertwined threads of genealogies – of historical forms expressed in language and spaces – that restrict the paths that can be taken towards the future.

We have to operate within this power, not as something that can be identified with specific places and individuals, but as a background that conditions all of them. For example, in front of a blank page we are not completely free to lay down our ideas. The set of words available to us and the grammar that articulates them, the suspicious or trusting audience waiting for our decisions or thoughts, the size of the page, how it can be reproduced and sent to others, our mother tongue and its relation to other languages, the registers of language such as orders, questions, prayers and pleas, our sleepy or alert states, our feelings of embarrassment or enthusiasm, our many different relations to an unconscious, all form a network of constraints: a form of power to work within, rather than a open field, or a void to be filled.

The role of transgression is to find the holes in the net of power or, in Foucault's words, to create a labyrinth where we can lose ourselves and become something else. He "writes in order to have no face" (AK: 19) because the face – identity – is a creation of history and part of the hold it has over us. Through our "faces", power operates on us and fixes the patterns we can move in. The role of Foucault's poststructuralism is to loosen the grip of power.

Free will and the philosophy of the subject cannot be the foundation for this resistance, because they are products of power, and because they are made by genealogies. Indeed, they are progeny of their most heavily determined lines. Foucault studies the transcendental conditions for free will, for the subject and for more common understanding of power (as power over, rather than as a pervasive historical conditioning). They are shown to be products rather than foundations. They are contingent, rather than necessary. They do not allow for true resistance, since they are intrinsic parts of forms of power.

This explains the comments on morality and policing towards the end of the passage quoted above. Foucault's impression is that freedom, organized around free subjects, is implicated in repression, organized around the identities that accompany that freedom. There is a damaging trade-off between a dependence on subjectivity and the role subjectivity plays in a network of power: "Do not ask me to remain the same: leave it to the bureaucrats and our police to see that our papers are in order" (AK: 19).

Foucault's work is therefore both Nietzschean, in its interest in genealogy and in power, and Kantian, in its interest in transcendental critique. He sees philosophical and political questions as a matter of a history of the emergence of forms of power, but also as inviting resistance through critique as the study and transgression of those forms. Two of his most important essays are therefore "Nietzsche, Genealogy, History" and "What is Enlightenment?" (both collected in *The Foucault Reader*). The first charts the debt that Foucault owes to Nietzsche; the second the debt to, but also the distance from Kant.

However, Foucault is neither fully Nietzschean nor Kantian. His merger of critique and genealogy raises new critical questions and exacerbates problems from both philosophies. In particular, *The Archaeology of Knowledge* tries to answer the following questions: how can history allow for openness? Why is power not so pervasive that it cannot be resisted? On what basis can we seek to transgress and criticize? What values are we to follow?

Continuity and discontinuity

In terms of history, the most important distinction introduced by Foucault in *The Archaeology of Knowledge* is the difference drawn between histories of continuity and of discontinuity. The distinction is important from two points of view: first, the new historian is a thinker of discontinuities; and secondly, history itself is discontinuous rather than continuous. The difference is crucial because it allows Foucault to think of genealogies as intrinsically loose rather than closed and fully determined. If history is discontinuous, then its hold on us is limited and fragmentary. We do not only inherit necessary forms and compulsions, but also gaps and opportunities. Spaces, words and identities are not hermetic things, but patchworks. Their looseness and incompleteness allows for opportunities for creation and variation. Openness is built into genealogy.

Furthermore, we are the product not of one history, but of many genealogies. These overlap and interact, so the sense that there can be a single overall correct account of the development of history must be replaced by many different accounts. These vary in terms of the current problems that they are related to and in terms of the points from whence they are told.

Foucault opposes two kinds of historians, around a distinction drawn between a new history of thought and an older history (although it is still operative in the present). Where the new history of thought seeks and discovers discontinuity, the older history moves towards ever more filled-in and monolithic structures: "In short, the history of thought, of knowledge, of philosophy, of literature seems to be seeking, and discovering, more and more discontinuities, whereas history itself appears to be abandoning the irruption of events in favour of stable structure" (AK: 6).

Foucault's point is more complicated that it first appears. He does not mean that there is a difference between discontinuous series in time and long continuous ones. as if history was either a long chain of necessary events or a series of detached ones. Rather, he means that the work of the historian can be distinguished in terms of whether it looks for and discovers stable or unstable structures, that is, in terms of what it retrieves from the past. Does the historian look for fixed elements that can be used as evidence for other things? Or does the historian look for unstable elements that are signs of the many different forces that came together to make them?

He explains this point further through the following reversal. History proper goes from the monument to the document; the new history goes from the document to the monument. A document is a stable structure and sign, whereas a monument is the coming together of many different tensions into something that always requires further interpretation.

A document would be something like a letter admitting guilt: a sign that confirmed a given theory. A monument would be something like a ruin from a bygone age: a complex aggregate of different remnants from that age. Historians of continuity try to turn monuments and their puzzles into usable documents, that is, into facts for a given thesis. Historians of discontinuity take things assumed to be facts and show how they are in fact still puzzling and open monuments. So the opposition is nowhere near as crude as it may have seemed. Neither historian presupposes a form of history; rather, they look at artefacts in different ways. The use of "seek", earlier, is itself a simplification and should be understood as a description of a series of theories, methods and forms of expected outcome. The new historian is an archaeologist in the sense that things from the past are assumed to be intrinsically puzzling, complex, irreducibly multifaceted objects, rather than forms of evidence.

This allows for a clarification in terms of Foucault's method. His philosophy leads to genealogies, that is, to intricate descriptions of the emergence, through history, of forms of power that operate in the present. But these genealogies are not monolithic continuities; they are constellations of discontinuities. Genealogy answers the questions: what conditioned evolution into this situation? How does it condition moves into the future? What acts are transgressions of this genealogy? Which ones merely strengthen its grip?

In turn, archaeology answers the questions: how do we trace a genealogy? What leads us to it? Which presuppositions render us blind to it or reveal it? Archaeology unearths and creates the material that allows us to trace genealogies. It is because this material takes the form of complex monuments that genealogies are not unitary and simple.

Foucault describes a series of important consequences that follow from this move to archaeology as the key method for genealogy:

- ruptures appear in the history of ideas and these contradict theses about long homogeneous historical periods;

- discontinuity becomes important in history, not as something to be overcome, but as a positive result in itself;
- global history is replaced by general history, that is, instead of seeking a total overview of history into which different histories can fit, we find many different histories that resist collection into a single overarching movement;
- methodological questions about the limits, levels and selection of objects of enquiry become more pressing.

It is worth signalling how these points intersect with a series of themes and problems from other poststructuralist thinkers. In the move from documents, as evidence for theories about long periods of history, to monuments, as complex points for different interpretations, Foucault questions the notion of the historical fact as origin and as vehicle for empirical verification or falsification. Instead of such facts, we have a troubling starting-point that makes theories about continuity and totality hard to sustain. It also makes it hard to define history as an empirical science modelled on the natural sciences. Instead, we are presented with a discontinuous history, in the poststructuralist sense of fragmented and heterogeneous. However, Foucault allows us to resist the naive version of this fragmentation: that it leads to completely separate units. Instead, we have complex interactions that resist a final totality. This is what he means by power: a web of influences across discontinuities.

Furthermore, it is not that Foucault simply denies enquiry into facts or the search for evidence; rather, his point is that such evidence cannot be found, unless we make false simplifications of the evidence. It is these simplifications that allow for the erroneous conclusion that facts support theses about long chains of necessary events within homogeneous histories.

These false simplifications also allow for the recognition of simple causal chains as opposed to complex networks. For Foucault, the statement "A caused B in the time-interval t_1–t_2" is at best an incomplete statement. Instead, we should have descriptions of genealogies alongside the archaeological interpretation of monuments: "Monument A can be interpreted as part of these emergent series through time bequeathing these limits and openings in the present". This is why he raises the methodological and theoretical problems of limits, levels and selections. Archaeology must not be seen as committed to objective views of evidence because the kind of fact required for objectivity does not exist. Instead, questions of rigour and objectivity are transferred from objects, facts or pieces of evidence, to the way in which these are set into series, classified into levels and included or excluded according to explicit principles of selection. The task of *The Archaeology of Knowledge* is to explain and justify Foucault's selections and classifications, not only in terms of the specific histories that he has worked on, but also, and more importantly, in terms of general principles.

This shift in history also changes the way we think in terms of justification and falsification. For example, the question is no longer whether a document is a justifiable verifier or falsifier of a theory (If X said Y, then she could not be accused of Z). Rather it is whether X is legitimately set into series with other pieces in order to give an account of an emergence (X, Y, Z, … chart the emergence of a new kind of criminal law). This is because explanations in terms of simple causal chains are less effective than explanations in terms of genealogies of power. There is never a single cause, but series of conditions.

Foucault highlights a further consequence of this shift. It, too, is a familiar theme of poststructuralism. The old history of continuities and documents still depends upon and supports the free subject. It still tends to anthropocentrism, humanism and to a division between material and human causality. This is because a monolithic causal account of history must posit a source of openness outside its closed chains of cause and effect if it wants to claim that things can be and could have been different. When asked "How come there is still the possibility of different outcomes?" or "Can we still hope for a different future?", historians committed to the causal account still answer, "Thanks to the acts of free subjects."

A source external to the great movements of causal history is given through the human subject:

> Continuous history is the indispensable correlative of the founding function of the subject: the guarantee that everything that has eluded him may be restored to him; the certainty that time will disperse nothing without restoring it in a reconstituted unity; the promise that one day the subject – in the form of historical consciousness – will once again be able to appropriate, to bring back under his sway, all those things that are kept at a distance by difference, and find what might be called his abode. (AK: 13)

Foucault's point is that continuity and the free subject are terrible twins, rather than opposed foes. The subject allows for an account of freedom and hence hope in apparently closed systems. But the predictability of the system allows for guarantees of positive outcomes, once the subject has intervened in it.

Foucault is critical of this ambiguous transcendence of subject and system, where the subject is both outside the causality and totality of the system, yet capable of acting within in it. It allows history to remain anthropocentric, that is, to be concerned principally with man's actions, psychology and capacities. It also remains humanistic, that is, it associates hope and actions towards the future with human values.

Against this foundational humanism, Foucault wants to defend a history where the human and human freedom are part of emergent genealogies, rather than independent of them. For him, hope and action are based within complex structures, rather than founded externally on the transcendence of the free subject: "But one must not be deceived: what is being bewailed with such vehemence is not the disappearance of history, but the eclipse of that form of history that was secretly, but entirely related to the synthetic activity of the subject …" (AK: 15). In line with other poststructuralist thinkers, Foucault associates the philosophical and historical error of transcendence with conservatism. Each time revolutionary thinkers, such as Marx and Nietzsche, put forward ways of thinking about history in terms of discontinuities, they are resisted. Forms of complex emergence and of evidence requiring multiple and open interpretation are rejected by a conservative move back to the continuity afforded by subjectivity and by histories based around subjects.

This reaction is in the name of continuous history. It is conservative because it turns the intrinsic difference and openness of history back on to secure chains of events, origins and documents. Liberating difference is then seen as something outside the system and not within it. It is restricted to humanism and to anthropocentrism, rather than to an open plurality of inflexions, evolutions and variations across series:

> The cry goes up that one is murdering history whenever, in a historical analysis – and especially if it is concerned with thought, ideas or knowledge – one is seen to be using in too obvious a way notions of threshold, rupture and transformation, the description of series and limits. (AK: 15)

It is therefore wrong to see Foucault as opposed to structuralism; rather, he wants to add to and develop the notion of structure in different ways and in terms of a new history. He shares the critique that structuralism affords in terms of notions of transcendence (nothing stands outside the structural differences, including man). Yet he thinks that the demands for principles regarding selections of series, in terms of levels and limits, call for different tools than those available in structuralism.

Finally, in terms of this discussion of continuity and discontinuity, it is important to make a very difficult, but ultimately crucial, distinction. When Foucault advocates discontinuity he must mean actual discontinuity that rests upon a transcendental continuity. He does not make this explicit and only Deleuze's metaphysics is sophisticated enough to make the point (hence the great interest in their debates and in Deleuze's important book on Foucault, as well as Foucault's shorter texts and remarks on Deleuze).

The distinction rests on the following problem. If all we have is actual discontinuity, then we return either to forms of transcendence (the discontinuities transcend one another), or to contradictions of interactions across discontinuities (they have effects on one another and they do not). So actual discontinuity has a transcendental condition: a continuity that relates actual discontinuities as things that connect, but noncausally and only at the level of principles rather than actual chains (see the discussion of reciprocal determination in Chapter 3, above).

Radical critique and the elements of history

When Foucault turns to new historical elements, to monuments rather than documents, and to discontinuity rather than continuity, how is he going to define these new historical elements? What is he going to archive, collect, comment on and set into theories? How is he going to justify his selections? What principles are at work in his new histories of madness, of disciplinary and clinical forms (for example, of prisons and punishments, of asylums, hospitals and medical treatments)?

In *The Archaeology of Knowledge* he develops a radical critique to answer these questions. This work is theoretical rather than practical. For Foucault, radical critique means the questioning of the limits and levels set by earlier histories. It also means a ceaseless application of that critique to the elements that come to replace them. Radical critique gives reasons for questioning the assumptions of given practices and theories. It proposes new selections resistant to this critique. Yet it subjects these new selections to a critique of their limits and presuppositions.

Foucault cannot arrive at a final theory, with final elements and methods. Instead, there is a twofold ethic: (i) to subject all theories and elements to critique concerning their presuppositions, in particular, regarding limits and levels; (ii) to create individual genealogies that maximize openness to new forms and practices without returning to earlier presuppositions. This ethic comes out very strongly in the three volumes of *The History of Sexuality*, where Foucault develops the idea of an aesthetics of existence.

Both aspects of this ethic explain why Foucault constantly emphasizes the temporary and mobile nature of his work. It is in movement and always working against itself, as well as against other returns to fixed presuppositions and values. Like Deleuze and Derrida, he is searching for ways to avoid constriction into norms and categories, but without having to fall back on to new norms and categories in avoiding others. This is as true for his historical works as it is for his more theoretical ones; both put theory and practice into question and transform it. Truths emerge, and they can be better grounded than others, in the sense of more resistant to current critical questions. But they are not final truths. They will fail the test of critique and yet, in so doing, they will have contributed to it and to the emergence of further truths.

Foucault develops his critical movement through a critique of a set of traditional historical objects. He calls this the negative part of his work. It frees up blockages to new ways of thinking by questioning and undermining unexamined presuppositions. Here are some of the main critical moves:

- Studies in terms of traditions, mentalities or spirits impose false boundaries on historical events. They create an illusory continuity by covering an underlying dispersal and complexity through reductive connections. *It is an event before it is a traditionally Scottish event. It is a complex way of thinking before it is reduced to a mentality. The age moves in many directions under the label of a particular spirit of the age.*
- Divisions in terms of discipline and genres are retrospective categories that often miss the much more varied and interconnected forms of the things they collect. Academics and artists are interdisciplinary before they are divided into separate faculties and art forms. Writing is many things (letter writing, political pleading, personal recollection) before it is retrospectively brought under a single and late banner such as "literature".
- The limits of the book are false. Books move beyond their edges and are dispersed into turns of phrase, concerns, debates and dialogues way beyond where they begin and end. The book is not necessarily the legitimate starting-point for thinking about this

dispersal and judging its significance; the dispersal is prior and the limit is imposed later.

- Bodies of work (oeuvres) organized around authors also presuppose false limits. The works include great varieties of forms and exclude other important ones or works (written by others, or deemed irrelevant): "As soon as one questions that unity, it loses its self-evidence; it indicates itself, constructs itself, only on the basis of a complex field of discourse" (AK: 26).
- It is not the case that history cannot access original events and that these events are somehow locked into inaccessible places such as private human intentions. The material available to historians is the event and it is a mistake to refer to an ungraspable origin: "Discourse must not be referred to the distant presence of the origin; it must be treated within the play of its instantiation" (AK: 28, translation modified).

It would be a mistake to read these points as advocating a complete break with one kind of material and a shift to another. Rather, Foucault is concerned with the assumptions regarding the limits of the material. He is not setting up simple oppositions. He is making a demand for further and deeper critical thought:

> They must not be rejected definitively of course, but the tranquillity with which they are accepted must be disturbed; we must show that they do not come about of themselves, but are always the result of a construction the rules of which must be known, and the justifications of which must be scrutinized: we must define in what conditions in view of which analyses certain of them are legitimate; and we must indicate which of them can never be accepted in any circumstances. (AK: 28)

Archaeology and genealogy are concerned with the hidden rules and justifications at work behind the selection of apparently obvious categories and objects. They seek to show how these rules and justifications have evolved. *The Archaeology of Knowledge* traces this evolution of rules about limits and questions its results. It attempts to replace falsifying limits with more careful and accurate ones. Here, falsifying means making false claims to final, prior or necessary limits and levels. For example, in describing relations between statements, Foucault charts moves between different hypotheses in terms of how to group them into sets, that is, into what he calls "discursive formations":

- We should move from the hypothesis that statements should be grouped according to the objects they refer to, and towards the hypothesis that they should be grouped according to how they disperse objects and separate them (by how far and following which rules). This is because the statements make the objects and not the contrary. The way they make the objects is varied and discontinuous; we encounter many objects and not one;
- We should move from the hypothesis that statements should be grouped according to their style and form, and towards the hypothesis that statements about different styles and forms should be charted in terms of how they came to be grouped, what orders emerged and in terms of what transformations. This is because disciplines such as medicine do not emerge with one style and form, but through the co-option of many;
- The hypothesis that statements can be grouped according to fundamental concepts at work in a given pursuit and discipline should be replaced by the hypothesis that we should follow the variation and dispersal of such grounds. This is because, in disciplines such as grammar, for example, we do not find a continuous line of coherent core concepts, but a variation in them and in the way they allow for other statements to be grouped;
- We should move from the hypothesis that statements should be grouped according to themes that correspond to disciplines, and towards the hypothesis that we should observe wide sets of strategic possibilities, that is, those moments where there is a choice between themes and directions for disciplines. This is because disciplines do not in fact correspond to long-lived themes; on the contrary, there are constant conflicts between them, changes of direction or periods of coexistence.

Foucault's argument here is empirical, that is, he is referring back to his earlier studies and to later studies in *The Archaeology of Knowledge* in order to support his points about changes in hypotheses. His initial hypotheses could not do justice to the complexity of the field and had to be replaced by others.

In his historical work, wherever Foucault sought unity, according to apparently sensible ways of grouping, he found dispersal. This led him to develop a new theoretical framework where statements were defined and grouped in a very bare and open form: a discursive formation based on statements. This is then defined as a way of bringing statements that describe a same dispersion together (for objects, styles, concepts and themes). It would be wrong to claim, therefore, that Foucault's philosophy is committed to a pointless and endless dispersal. Its significance as critique is to accept that there are dominant forms, such as the initial hypotheses questioned above. It then questions these forms by bringing out the many coalitions that undermine the forms, with as much precision as possible. Dispersion is absent both in the acceptance of the first thing open to critique and in the crucial principle that critique brings together that which affords the first critical dispersal, even if this is then to be criticized in turn.

Foucault's history is therefore concerned with patterns of sameness around differences or points of inflection and change. He looks not for what continues through history, but what evolves and becomes other. This becoming is charted and explained by looking for similarities around the points of change, bringing together what had not been brought together before. The new historians are not concerned about finding A at epoch E_1 and again at epoch E_2; rather, they bring together all the influences around a difference in E_1 and E_2 in order to understand what generates those differences and how they are significant for us now. They seek out the rules of formation for these new similarities, that is, the conditions that allow for the change and for the coming together of disparate statements. They search for what made this becoming possible, not so much in terms of direct causes, but in terms of why those causes themselves were possible: "The rules of formation are conditions of existence (but also of coexistence, maintenance, modification, and disappearance) in a given discursive field" (AK: 42).

For example, we cannot explain the emergence of a new phenomenon in history through a privileged object (the "new" madness, or clinical practice, or economic form of exchange). Instead, having noted the many forms hidden within such objects, the historian should seek out the different rules and relations that allowed for these various objects to be formed and identified. Object A turns out to be an illusory cloak thrown over *a, b, c, d, e.* But each of these emerged and were brought together thanks to similarities between different rules governing their formation (where a rule must not be understood as necessarily legal or formal, but rather as that which made practices permissible and possible, or not).

For example, when a new musical genre is identified (rap, jazz, punk), it is a label imposed over a series of differences and loose similarities. This imposition becomes clear and is made clear as the new historian charts the many subdivisions (East Coast/West Coast, fusion/original, rock-oriented/electro-oriented, political/pop …) But these are then brought together again through a study of the similarities between the "rules" that allowed them to appear (for example, the rules around statements about disaffection, race, free time, greater wealth, new poverty, revolution, new instruments, moves across borders, dominance of labels and so on). So the interviews with musicians, while destroying historical hopes for a same homogeneous object ("reggae", "indie") still provide series of statements that chart the multi-stranded emergence of a more complex thing.

Instead of seeking out objects, styles, concepts and themes, the historian should work through texts in order to find ways of grouping statements around diversions in terms of objects, styles, concepts and strategies. When did musicians begin to move away from a particular instrument and style? When were root concepts and themes rebelled against and which statements stand for this rebellion?

Progressive politics in poststructuralism: anything goes?

Foucault's search for unity only in dispersion and his focus on points of change rather than continuity lends his history and philosophy a politically progressive edge. This is because it is directed towards the emergence of new differences, rather than sameness, and because it uncovers a hidden dispersal under apparent continuity. His work allows for resistance to false generalizations based on history, or based on concepts that are supposed to be extra-historical, but that have political roots. After Foucault, generalizations about madness, sexuality and gender lose their impact in the face of strong criticisms.

First, each of these forms is shown to be much more complex than often thought. There are not two sexes but many (as Foucault shows in his work on hermaphrodites, for example, in *Herculine Barbin* (1978)). Madness is shown to be multiformed and to take on very complicated relations with power structures, values and forms of production. This explains Foucault's distance from both Freudian psychoanalysis and strictly biochemical brain-based accounts of madness. Neither captures the full complexity and historicity of madness or of their own historical emergence and stakes. It is interesting to contrast this approach with Kristeva's greater reliance on Freud (see Chapter 6).

In his work on the history of sexuality, Foucault follows aesthetics of existence as they evolve and change in relation to power. Sexuality – that is, relations between bodies, desires and pleasures, rather than sex or gender – is created in multiple ways, none of which can claim to be prior. It is formed indirectly through decisions about the self, as well as by historical forces well beyond our control. Foucault's work is central to sexual liberalization, openness and tolerance because it counters appeals to fixed states, hierarchies and values. It provides important material for political studies in these areas, by allowing them to unmask false appeals to essences or to nature. There is no independent essence or nature. Both are historical and part of ongoing and open power relations. Hence any appeal to high moral values based on these unchanging forms lacks any merit.

Secondly, each of the social forms studied in Foucault's books is not only shown to be essentially historical in the sense of essentially past, but also shown to be the product of interrelated genealogies and struggles between forms of power and creative openings in the present and directed to the future. *The only thing that is essential is the historical and future-driven movement of gathering and dispersal – of discontinuities and oblique interactions.* Not only is there is no natural division of sex and sexuality, nor essential distinctions between madness and reason, there is also no one true history of their becoming or evolution. There are no essential definitions of race, gender, health, sanity or human life that would allow for eternally just behaviours to them. But neither is there a single historical logic that would provide at least some kind of certainty and a return to distinctions and values that we could be sure of.

Foucault's history strengthens the defence of immanence in post-structuralism. His account of immanence also resists any account of its own internal logic, through its insistence on the complex and open form of history. It thereby allows for a critique of transcendent values and forms on historical grounds, alongside a critique of accounts of necessary historical processes. To impose such transcendence or single logic in immanence is in fact to be radically unjust and to deny the openness of history in the name of false and violent idols. This adds further explanations for Foucault's important role for many contemporary movements of resistance and liberation. His work allows for stands against discrimination on the basis of sex (we are not necessarily of one sex or the other). It allows for an affirmation of homosexuality as an aesthetic of existence and as a complex historical movement that resists the false labels of "unnatural" or "deviant".

His work shows the illegitimate violence that has been perpetrated on those judged as mad, as abnormal, as "lower", or "outsiders". It gives us methods and material for showing this injustice, by tracing its basis and historical provenance. More importantly, by opening up fields, by showing their evolution, but also their complexity, openness and discontinuity, Foucault teaches us that the future is open and can only be worked with in truthful manner if its openness and variability are affirmed through the way we live. An aesthetics of existence is an experimentation with the positive differences that lie within structures of power.

A serious political accusation against Foucault can be denied at this point. He is not reactionary. Nor does his position imply a return to reactionary politics. His commitment to the critique of false claims to universality, essences and naturalness is a grounds for a politics of tolerance and openness, since it refuses all exclusions on false grounds (as demonstrated historically) and since it is committed to similar critiques of any return to false values in its own practice.

This self-critical aspect of his work is reflected in his style through its emphasis on questions and enquiry at every turn. Foucault's books do not arrive at conclusions without bringing them into question. The same is true of any given movement, entity or event. His method is committed to examining each one for further ramifications and discontinuities, rather than allowing for the setting of a new orthodoxy. Yet four related philosophical criticisms lie in wait for this critical political resistance and creativity:

- What kind of historical facts is Foucault's work dependent upon? If it is not dependent on any notion of fact, then it seems to be an "anything goes" subjective account of history with no claim to truth. If it is dependent on some kind of core facts, does this not contradict his points on openness and diversity?
- What is the relation of Foucault's work to science and to scientific theories and data? Do not scientific sources carry more weight than loose historical observations, for example, with respect to sex and to sexuality, or to clinical conditions such as madness? If Foucault ignores the superior value of such sources, does it not invalidate his claims in spheres where there is substantial scientific knowledge?
- What is the basis for Foucault's account of the discontinuity of history? If that basis lies in empirical historical observation, then he is not in a position to discount discoveries of continuity or abstract rational justifications for it. If the basis does not lie in empirical work, then he is working in contradiction to his main theses by positing something extra-historical.
- Is the account of the discontinuity of history not a claim to some kind of continuity, not so much from the point of view of

justification (as in the previous criticism) but from the point of view of the types and forms of discontinuity? History is discontinuous in a particular way. This way gives it a form of continuity and a method for establishing relations across discontinuities.

In short, Foucault's work requires careful reflection on its claims to historical truth and on its relation to science. It is open to questions regarding its empirical basis in terms of the Humean problem of induction (broadly, that repetition of a pattern in the past cannot guarantee repetition in the future). It seems to rest on the paradox that identifying a difference or a discontinuity is a way of bridging them and establishing identities and continuities.

This explains why *The Archaeology of Knowledge* spends so much time on the theory of archaeology, in relation to questions of evidence, fact, contradiction, justification and science. Put simply, Foucault's arguments are that there are basic historical functions – statements – but that these do not impose a positive content or meaning on history, only a positive function. This function is a relation between discourse and objects. Statements allow for the tracing of complex relations between what is said and what is seen, to the point where we can begin to speak positively of genealogies or emergent relations that hold between ideas and things. The function is a drawing together of relations.

Foucault's historical method can be traced out in bare form from his work on statements. We can draw two important consequences from the key definition that a statement is a function, that is, something that sets up relations between other things, rather than a positive thing in itself. Both consequences allow for answers to the criticisms set out above.

First consequence of the definition of statements

The definition means that Foucault avoids a positive fixed definition of statements. A statement is not a proposition (a logical form) or a sentence (a grammatical form) or an utterance (something said by a subject). Each of these would set down presuppositions for the form of evidence to be used. For example, Foucault shows how there can be statements that are not logical, but that have a function, that is, an historical effect (a contradiction, for instance). He shows how statements can exist (symbols, for instance) yet not fit the grammatical form of the sentence. He shows how some statements work as functions yet cannot be defined as someone's intentional utterance (a random list, for instance).

This resistance to a positive definition of statements as independent entities is very important, since it avoids the imposition of extra-historical conditions on what can stand as historical evidence (that it should have a logical form; that it should have a grammatical form, that it should be thought of in terms of human actors or subjects). Foucault shows that each of these is itself historical: it changes through time. He also shows that each excludes significant historical events.

But if statements are not positive things that can be identified as such, what are they? Here is the key definition:

> I now realise that I could not define the statement as a unit of linguistic type (superior to the phenomenon of the word, inferior to the text); but that I was dealing with an enunciative function that involved various units (these may sometimes be sentences, sometimes propositions; but the are sometimes made up of fragments of sentences, series or tables of signs, a set of propositions or equivalent formulations); and, instead of giving a "meaning" to these units, this function relates them to a field of objects; instead of providing them with a subject, it opens them up for a number of positive subjective positions; instead of fixing their limits, it places them in a domain of coordination and coexistence; instead of determining their identity, it places them in a space in which they are used and repeated. (AK: 119)

So a statement sets up a relation between linguistic units and fields of objects. The role of the historian is then twofold: it is to find the (rare) statements that allow such relations to be traced; but it is also to convey the openness and ongoing variation proper to the function.

This is why Foucault speaks of archaeology. Archaeology is the unearthing of key statements in their richness and their patterns of repetition and transformation amid a wealth of documentation. It asks these questions: what are the key statements here? How do they determine relations between different texts, utterances and signs (the "said")? How do they determine relations between different objects (in the very wide sense or anything visible or sensible, a building, a tool, a sound, a feeling – the "seen")? And, most importantly, how do they determine ongoing historical transformations between the texts and objects?

Two remarks follow from this initial definition of historical work. First, it is not the case that Foucault's method is a case of "anything goes". It allows for failure: the function might not appear. Secondly, it allows for judgements regarding relative success in terms of scope, rigour and relevance. The following questions show the limits and criteria that apply to the method. How far does the function range (both through time and spatially)? How convincing is argument for the constituent relations? How strong are those relations in terms of the contemporary forms they are supposed to be related to?

Second consequence of the definition of statements

It is not the case that there are no positive elements that can be appealed to and judged in objective terms. The archaeologist is committed to the following questions and can be criticized for answering them badly. Did the said and the seen appealed to and set in relation really exist? What evidence is there for them? Is it robust? Foucault's historical works are careful studies of texts and of objects. At times, that work can be shown to be incomplete or to involve errors. At times, it can be shown to be unconvincing in tracing relations and in articulating evidence. This is an entirely good thing, since it subjects the work to criteria that guard against a vague relativism and a disregard for thorough research.

In relation to statements, discourse and objects, Foucault is a positivist: they exist; we can examine them; they are open to question. Yet his positivism is not a pure objectivity, in the sense, for example, of a history that claimed merely to lay out facts free of interpretation, or in the sense of a history that claimed to be able to verify theories in a quasi-scientific manner (*these historical facts prove this theory*). Instead, the selection of the statements and the setting up of the functions is inherently open to question and to interpretation.

Readers must then ask themselves whether they are convinced by these selections, not only in the sense of the evidence, but in the sense of their effectiveness in relation to contemporary problems. Does Foucault's history of madness, does any archaeology, have important points to bring to contemporary debates and problems, not in a general sense, but from the singular point of view of a thinker or set of thinkers grappling with a given problem? Even within these apparently subjective questions, there are criteria and bases for judgements. In the above passage, the openness and lack of fixity of the functions is given great importance. Resistance to identity and a usefulness and repeatability within new situations are to be valued. This explains Foucault's remarks against interpretation, meaning and subjects; these would limit both the use and the openness by bending them to dominant meanings and actors.

The justification for these further criteria lies in the form of the statement. It would be betrayed by a return to fixed meanings and to the control of subjects, since this would set up a prior way of organizing and selecting statements. But why would this be a wrong way of proceeding? Is Foucault's work turning in ever greater circles that evade the central question of whether we should appeal to certain core foundations, such as the human subject and scientific objectivity, or core values, such as human freedom?

No. Foucault's books are careful examinations of our dominant presuppositions. They seek to show how meaning is historical. They seek to convince us of the limits of the subject as a ground for truth, values and knowledge. His poststructuralism is anti-foundational, but on the basis of extensive research on possible foundations and arguments against their necessity.

The challenge, then, is to read his work and to judge whether his studies successfully resist the imposition of such foundations and values. His books have the great merit of remaining open and of explicitly leaving judgements to "a number of positive subjective positions". This does not mean that these positions can ignore the positive criteria outlined above. To be true to Foucault is to read him critically and to be critical of our own positions.

Poststructuralism as archaeology: science and knowledge

Foucault's positivism gives methods and criteria for success and failure to his work. However, this does not mean that his history and philosophy are sciences or modelled on the sciences. They do not involve the same restrictions on what can count as evidence, nor the same demands for theories to stand in relation to one another through systematically regulated claims to truth (for example, in terms of falsification). Archaeology and the genealogies that it produces are looser and wider ranging than scientific theories. Does this imply that Foucault should be criticized for being unscientific?

He raises and answers a version of this objection in the final sections of *The Archaeology of Knowledge*. The answer is all important, since it involves a definition of knowledge as something more than scientific knowledge. However, for this distinction to work it is important to extend the concept of knowledge to take account of Foucault's choice of vocabulary.

"*Savoir*" is the French noun used by Foucault. It can be translated as knowledge or as learning. The former is the option taken – rightly

– by the translator of *The Archaeology of Knowledge*. Yet the French verb "*savoir*" has more meanings than "to know". It also stresses some meanings of "to know" more strongly. In particular, with respect to questions of science, "*savoir*" does not only mean "knowing X", "knowing that" or "understanding that" (all sometimes rendered better through the verb "*connaître*"); it also means "understanding how", "being informed of" and "knowing how".

Foucault's choice of words therefore allows him to argue that there is an important form of knowledge (*savoir* as opposed to *connaître/connaissance*) that lies somewhat outside the domain of the sciences, yet is still important and worth pursuing. Thanks to the sciences we "know that" but this still requires a more open and singular "knowing how". More importantly, he will also claim that this other form of knowledge affords valuable critical insights on science that are not available from within science proper. Science needs history, not only as some kind of record, but as a live critical tool.

The distinction is therefore at the core of Foucault's argument because it allows him to claim that there is knowledge (*savoir*) before sciences have become well formed: as a "knowing how" on the way to a "knowing that". It also allows him to argue that this formation must be understood on the basis of archaeology (through the claim that this knowing how is not completely accessible to science). Finally, it allows him to defend the view that the point of such archaeology is not to give an account that serves the emergence of true sciences and true knowledge. On the contrary, there is a positive and important role for archaeology alongside and critical of any given science.

The detailed steps of Foucault's arguments are important because they clarify the basis for his distance from the sciences. They are as follows:

1. It takes time for scientific disciplines to emerge. There is therefore a time of pre-disciplinary evolution where the notion of the discipline cannot account for the historical event of its own emergence. Disciplinary rules, norms and practices cannot be applied to the processes that give rise to them. The positive statements, forms of discourse and objects sought by the archaeologist will not necessarily be those of the discipline. These things range much wider and involve looser relations and conflicts than the tightly regulated rules of the discipline. For example, in the case of psychiatry: "the discursive formation whose existence was mapped by the psychiatric discipline was not coextensive with it, far from it: it went well beyond the boundaries of psychiatry" (AK: 197).

2. An archaeology is not validated by showing how different events led to a dominant and settled scientific discipline. This is because the historical process involves overlaps between different disciplines and forms that do not fall under them. Therefore, any account that subjects a particular series of historical events to a single discipline, falsely excludes others and excludes extra-scientific events that were important in the evolution, although these may now be insignificant or even inadmissible from the point of view of the final discipline:

> Discursive formations are not, therefore, future sciences at the stage at which, still unconscious of themselves, they are quietly being constituted: they are not, in fact, in a state of teleological subordination in relation to the orthogenesis of the sciences. (AK: 199)

3. This relative independence from individual sciences does not mean that archaeology and resulting genealogies are independent of the sciences: as a "non-science" of that which is itself unscientific. On the contrary, they can feed into and study changes in well-formed mature sciences; for example, when a discipline splits into others, or when influences from outside a discipline's tightly defined rules has an effect on its development and on its rules. This does not mean that the archaeologist has to claim that the sciences are scientifically right to have split or changed. It means that there are positive things to be observed that show that changes have occurred, where they have occurred and in terms of which relations. Any judgements must follow the historian's tracing of that occurrence.

These points lead Foucault to describe knowledge/*savoir* as opposed to scientific knowledge. The former is a grouping of different elements, not according to a pre-set scientific rule, but in order to explain and trace the emergence of such rules. Where the scientist may ask "Was this experiment conducted according to the proper rules of the subject?", the archaeologist asks "How and where did such rules emerge? What principles of selection were involved? What was rejected? What different influences were held together? Which statements mark the passage from one system to another?" So the relative looseness of archaeological *savoir* is not a complete lack of rules or topic. On the contrary, it is a rigorous response to the problem of how to draw knowledge from a diverse and heterogeneous material:

> To analyse positivities is to show in accordance with which rules a discursive practice may form groups of objects, enunciations, concepts or theoretical choices. The elements thus formed do not constitute a science with a defined structure of ideality; their system of relations is certainly less strict; but neither are they items of knowledge piled up on one another, derived from heterogeneous experiments, traditions, or discoveries, and linked only by the identity of the subject that possesses them. (AK: 200)

Knowledge/*savoir* must be a grouping, rather than a straightforward rejection of that which does not fit specified rules, because many different incompatible influences shape a science (or any form traced by a genealogy). The scientist rightly ignores illegitimate data, those based on superstition or religious belief, for example. But the archaeologist must be able to take account of the religious and anti-religious context of the emergence of a science. For Foucault, science and archaeology have different domains. There is a place for both.

But should that really be so? Would it not be better to concentrate on the sciences in their mature form, to forget their mixed history and benefit from and protect their well-regulated practices? Why bother with histories when we have the benefits of their term? Or – to show the absurdity of Foucault's position – should we advocate that everything become archaeology, with no place for science? His answer to these objections is that, although there is a difference in domain, this does not mean that the two forms of knowledge do not have a role to play for one another. This is the case for archaeology, where the discoveries of the sciences and their rules for evidence and proof are central to verifying what Foucault calls "positivities" (discourses and objects). It is not that archaeology should discount carbon dating or scientifically based proofs of authorship. The issue beyond science is how these positivities are to be grouped to describe complexes of power.

This issue is also, though, the reason why we cannot merely stay within established sciences, free of worries about their tainted emergence and of the way it bathes in extra-scientific forms of power and wild mixtures of contradictory forces. A science must rejoin discourse, politics, society, objects beyond its direct scope, speculation, emotions, desires. It must interact with what Foucault calls "ideology". When it does so its genealogy matters again, because it has to operate outside the boundaries of its own regulations and in the sphere traced by the archaeologist.

Foucault's poststructuralism is not anti-science. On the contrary, it seeks an extension of science into other discourses and it seeks to explain the role of science in the emergence of forms of power, not as a negative force, but as one that cannot be free of ideology. This is not the crude and mistaken argument that scientific method is necessarily ideological. Rather, it is the point that science matters because it can take an important place among many other practices, but there are no final overarching rules for right and wrong ways of taking that place.

six

Poststructuralism, psychoanalysis, linguistics: Julia Kristeva's *Revolution in Poetic Language*

Revolution and poststructuralism

Julia Kristeva's *Revolution in Poetic Language* [*La revolution du langage poétique*] first appeared in French in 1974. It was translated in much abridged form in 1984. The abridgement is no doubt due to the great length and scope of the original text, which had 640 very dense pages. Like Deleuze's *Difference and Repetition* and Lyotard's *Discours, figure*, the book is Kristeva's long thesis for a French doctorate (*doctorat d'état*). The three books are testament to the very high quality achieved in this now less prevalent form of academic work. Indeed, a consideration of the change from long, relatively rare and immensely time-consuming works to shorter more standardized ones would benefit from a poststructuralist study as to the forces at work and the values that are slipping away to be replaced by others.

The French title should be understood as "the revolution *of* poetic language" as well as "revolution *in* poetic language". This is because Kristeva does not only believe that there is a revolution in poetry and literature towards the end of the nineteenth century (with Mallarmé and Lautréamont), but that this revolution and later ones in twentieth-century literature (with Joyce, Artaud and Pound) constitute a social, linguistic and political revolution. Her thesis is therefore much more than a claim about a dramatic change in art. It is a claim about the revolutionary power of art. The main support for this claim lies in the view that, by challenging and changing language, art can reveal and shake wider political and social structures. *Only by achieving a revolution in language can we achieve a revolution in society.*

For Kristeva, a key aspect of this revolution lies in its capacity to show how language is dominated by male structures, desires and forms of thought. *Her revolution is a feminist revolution – not exclusively, yet essentially.* She makes this clear in the fiery conclusion to the book (cut in the translation):

> As soon as this power is recognised as such, it situates itself on the side of the symbolic, of institutions, apparatuses, structures that recognise no "feminine specificity" and that subordinate the problematic of reproduction to that of production. In this symbolic space, mother-woman is consequently either denied or fetishised: her self-possessed enjoyment is objectified, exchanged and lost. (RPL: 613)

Language and society are male-dominated, not only nor most importantly by actual men, but by ways of representing, of organizing, of working and of structuring that are male. The very fact that this gendering of forms of representation and organization is denied shows the exclusion of woman, that is, of specifically feminine forms, or more properly of feminine processes.

The quote marks around "feminine specificity" in the above passage indicate the problem that Kristeva is working with, since she does not mean a physical form or the historically male-dominated senses of the feminine; quite the contrary. "Feminine specificity" must be understood in terms of sexuality, sexual reproduction and enjoyment, in the complicated sense captured by the French word *jouissance* (enjoyment, sexual pleasure, pleasure in possession, orgasm). But how can Kristeva argue for this specificity and for its artistic, social and revolutionary power? Should not a concept such as "woman" be understood in language in terms of its historical and actual senses, and should not women be understood through the concept? How else could they be understood? If there is a feminist revolution to be achieved, should it not refer to concrete ideas and forms, rather than make claims to something ineffable that stands outside them?

Kristeva's book is a carefully argued response to these questions. It is also a critique of their basis. Her argument takes two routes. *First, using psychoanalysis, she studies processes that lie outside language, but that are presupposed by it and that it depends upon. Secondly, she shows that this dependence leaves language open to internal revolutionary trans-*

formations. It is possible to release the underlying processes back into language; this is their revolutionary potential.

This release focuses on the psychoanalytic process of negation and on the place for poetic revolution within language. Poetic revolution draws out the negation necessary in language, that is, the necessity for it to deny its condition in unconscious processes and in their resistance to its well-ordered forms. According to Kristeva, well-determined language follows from a negation and rejection of a prior set of processes that are disordered and disordering, at least form the point of view of what constitutes truth and sense in language.

In order to make sense out of a multiplicity of contradictory drives and possibilities, language imposes an order by negating some of them; for example, by rejecting them as nonsense, or as involving objects that cannot be referred to, or as contradictory to necessary presuppositions of language (in terms of grammar or dialogical forms). This policing of language is a negation of the multiple processes that it emerges out of.

However, language is also a negation of negation or of that policing function because language is affirmed to be natural, or true, or only to make any sense if it takes a certain form. It is then denied that other possibilities have to be negated in the sense of a competition between impulses and desires. Rather, they are denied in the deeper and more duplicitous sense of not existing, or of not being possible, of being self-contradictory or illusory. This second denial is the negation of negation.

In response to this double-negation – the negation of the pre-linguistic unconscious and then the negation of that negation – poetic revolution introduces those processes back into language. This is done by refusing forms of order, truthfulness, reference, grammar and dialogue (the position of the subject, for example). An apparent nonsense, ungrammaticality or contradiction of grammatical rules is shown to operate in language. It is shown to have an effect and to interact with well-ordered language.

Despite breaking with accepted form, poetic language sets off effects through other forms of language. It begins a revolution in them, in the sense of giving new forms to them, of infusing them with rejected desires and, in turn, of forcing them to reject them more overtly or order them into new but manageable forms and desires. For example, when poets break with standard grammar, introducing new and contradictory forms, they set off a revolutionary process, rather than merely produce examples of an indigestible nonsense:

> The text is able to explore the mechanism of rejection in its heterogeneity because the text is a practice that pulverises

unity, making it a process that posits and displaces theses. In other words, the text exposes, for representation, the extreme moment characteristic of all processes as practice.

(RPL: 208, translation modified)

By heterogeneity of rejection, Kristeva means the double aspect of nega-tion (its refusal and refusal of refusal). Revolutionary literary practice is a process of change, rather than an apparently simple, well-ordered mechanism (in a "straightforward" functional linguistic exchange, for instance).

To show this duplicitous mechanism, the poetic text resists and breaks the unity imposed through claims to order language. It shows each thesis on language to be breakable and invites it to be replaced (hence the need for ongoing revolution):

In every kind of society and situation, the text's function is therefore to lift the repression that weighs heavily on this moment of struggle. It is a function that particularly threatens or dissolves the bond between subject and society, but simul-taneously creates the conditions for its renewal.

(RPL: 208, translation modified)

The demand for order in language is particularly repressive ("Your claims to truth must take this form. You must speak in this way, to have made sense. You will not have said anything of worth unless it is in this grammatical form.") Revolutionary poetry shows that each of these forms of repression can be overcome.

In so doing, however, it also undermines the link between subject and society, in so far as the connection depends on that order. That is, the subject is a product of the social order (rather than a condition for it). It therefore falls when the order is challenged. Furthermore, that order is often best challenged by challenging the form, value and necessity of the subject.

This is not a destructive challenge to the possibility of any society. On the contrary, *Kristeva works towards a dialectical relation between language and extra-linguistic drives and between the language of poetic revolution and well-ordered language.* Each of the terms presupposes the other. Language is necessary for the expression of drives, while presupposing them. The subject and society are necessary forms for poetic revolution, both for it to take place and as part of its future ordering.

The poetic revolution forces language to change, adapt, open up and enter into a dialectical relation with unconscious processes. It also explains the intensity and significance of language, that is, how different senses and claims to truth have a grip on us in terms of desires. The revolution is therefore a permanent one that brings negation and transformation together in a dialectics: an ongoing opening up, then closing down of productive disorder in language.

Like Lyotard and Deleuze, Kristeva shows unconscious presuppositions behind common views of knowledge, in particular, knowledge about language in its relation to the world. This appeal to an unconscious allows for an explanation of why language matters to us, over and above what it is and how it works. Here, "to matter" is much more than to fulfil an important technical role, in the sense of allowing us to achieve certain ends. It means to set us in motion, to drive us to act, to disturb and to give pleasure, to be the object of fetishes, destruction and creativity. *Primarily, poetic revolution is about language as object of desire and not about language as tool. But it is also the release of desire into the only apparent neutrality of technique and function.*

Poststructuralism and language: the semiotic and the symbolic

But how does Kristeva justify this appeal to extra-linguistic processes? How can she demonstrate that these processes exist and that they undermine traditional ideas about language? Why does there need to be an understanding of language in relation to desire or to unconscious impulses? Why is it not sufficient to seek to refine the ways in which language allows us to make sense to one another and to refer to things in the world? These questions bring out two aspects of Kristeva's work that make her stand out.

First, among poststructuralists, she is perhaps the most dependent on Freudian psychoanalysis. Thanks to Freudian and Lacanian ideas and interpretations, Kristeva is able to study processes, such as negation in language, as well as pre-conscious and unconscious drives. This has the great strength of providing an extensive theoretical basis for her appeal to processes, something that is sometimes lacking in other poststructuralist thinkers. However, it invites the great range of critical reactions to Freud from many different camps.

Secondly, *Revolution in Poetic Language* provides the most comprehensive study of linguistics of any poststructuralist work. This is because

Kristeva seeks to demonstrate how a very wide range of theories of language presuppose and yet deny extra-linguistic processes. The range includes structuralism (notably, Lévi-Strauss, Hjelmslev and Jakobson) phenomenology (Husserl), analytic theories of language (Frege) and contemporary linguistics (notably Chomsky). She spends time showing how each theory must be complemented by her own appeal to pre-linguistic processes. This accounts in part for the length of the book, but also for its still underestimated critical richness. It also explains Kristeva's wide influence and her important position among contemporary theorists of language. However, the book is not solely theoretical; on the contrary, in the original French it is split into two parts, where the longer latter part is an application of the earlier theory (this latter work on Mallarmé, Lautréamont and Artaud – among others – is also omitted from the English translation).

This theory–application structure and commitment to a wide range of new theoretical terms (both linguistic and psychoanalytic) is problematic from the point of view of poststructuralism as developed elsewhere. The other works studied here put greater emphasis on practice in relation to theory, that is, theory only emerges as a practice. With Kristeva, this is not the case, at least in the early works. The theory and practice split remains with its virtue in allowing for a clear definition of language and of its conditions to emerge, but also with its vice in inviting criticisms of the concepts created by Kristeva in terms of their dependence on foundational claims, for example, in terms of her dependence on Freud.

For Kristeva, there is a revolutionary poetic, social and political practice. This is dialectical, ongoing and constantly transforming itself. However, there is also a theoretical apparatus that remains independent of that practice and that gives it a specific form, for example in terms of the classification of drives into negative and positive. This theory is itself dialectical, in the sense that any separation and opposition of drives also involves their conjunction and interdependence. However, the two dialectics are not fused and theory and practice can still be seen as separate in Kristeva in a way inconsistent with Derrida's deconstruction, for example.

The basis for her theory is a distinction drawn between the semiotic and the symbolic. In simple terms, the former can be associated with pre-linguistic drives and the latter with well-ordered language. However, since Kristeva goes on to characterize both realms in terms of processes rather than objects, it is important to note that the semiotic involves processes that go from itself into the symbolic. It is equally important to note that the reverse is true: processes in the symbolic extend into the semiotic and are a crucial part of it. This relation of the two realms is key to understanding Kristeva's linguistics, since it extends into all aspects of her work in two ways. First, it allows her to develop criticisms of any linguistics that denies one or the other realm. In practice, this leads to a critique of the denial of the semiotic in linguistics, and of the denial of the symbolic in very extreme poetic practices that embrace a destructive madness.

Secondly, it allows her to study any given form in terms of its relation to both realms. For example, the subject (the human subject) is "always both semiotic and symbolic, no signifying system he produces can be 'exclusively' semiotic or 'exclusively' symbolic, and is instead necessarily marked by an indebtedness to both" (RPL: 24). This means that Kristeva rejoins other poststructuralists in not fitting the false caricature of being simply "anti-subject". On the contrary, *the subject is a necessary form and is only opposed when it is defined as a primary foundation, when it fact it is a result of semiotic and symbolic processes.*

Kristeva defines the semiotic in a number of different ways. All owe a debt to Freud, not least because the semiotic must be understood as disposition of drives, energies or primary processes. The semiotic is the field where these drives come together in series of relations of displacement and condensation, that is, where they work together, prior to having an effect on fixed actual forms. Unconscious drives have a series of relations before they work on consciousness and before they can be said to work in linguistic forms. This is the semiotic. Kristeva gives the field a specific term, the semiotic *chora*, "to denote an essentially mobile and extremely provisional articulation constituted by movements and their ephemeral stases" (RPL: 25). This first definition is both difficult and hard to relate to more familiar forms. It is therefore helpful to insist on two further ways of understanding the semiotic *chora*. First, it is presupposed by familiar forms and can be described through them, for example in terms of the subject:

> Discrete quantities of energy move through the body of the subject who is not yet constituted as such and, in the course of his development, they are arranged according to the various constraints imposed on this body – always already involved in a semiotic process – family and other processes.   (RPL: 25)

This energy can be understood as a set of desires or drives that have not yet been organized, for example, when they are present in a very young child (Kristeva studies Freudian theories of child development in depth in *Revolution in Poetic Language*). Yet despite this lack of organization, the drives are related.

The drives form and undo relations. They essay different connections, only a few of which will be set in later imposed organizations. This disorganized set of relations is the *chora*: "In this way the drives, which are 'energy' charges as well as 'psychical' marks, articulate what we call a chora: a non-expressive totality formed by the drives and their stases in a motility that is as full of movement as it is regulated" (RPL: 25). *The semiotic is at once the source of our movements (energy), in the sense of attractions, and the source of our burgeoning mental states (psychical marks).*

The chora is "non-expressive" in the sense that it is not a structure that has a deeper meaning. It is not a system of signs that refers to something outside itself. Nor, though, does it have a structural stability that would allow sense to emerge as a series of fixed repeated relations, hence Kristeva's insistence on motility (movement and regulation where neither gains the upper hand). This movement and resistance to structure and external reference is all-important, since otherwise the *chora* could be defined as another language, either through the things it refers to, or through its inner set of fixed relations. Instead, the *chora* resists all such systematic identification; its identity is fleeting and any instance of it fails due to its ongoing movements. This lack of identity raises a serious objection through the question of how we know the semiotic *chora* is there at all. What is the evidence for it? How is it deduced? It is a mere fiction, or are there stronger reasons for believing in its existence?

The answer to these questions is that the semiotic *chora* is posited and confirmed only through an analysis of its effects. This explains Kristeva's debt to Freudian psychoanalysis, not only in terms of its claims to unconscious drives, but in its clinical studies of such drives, through dreams or compulsions, for example, and through its theories about infantile sexuality.

Revolution in Poetic Language is dependent on careful and up-to-date psychoanalytic theories and studies. Its work extends beyond Freud to studies of Lacan and Klein. This does not mean that the book is strictly a work of psychoanalysis, but it means that its main arguments follow psychoanalytical theories very closely (as one might expect from a practising psychoanalyst such as Kristeva). This reliance on Freud and psychoanalysis is significant because is distinguishes Kristeva's work from other poststructuralists (notably, from Deleuze's critical stance in his *Anti-Oedipus*, written with Félix Guattari; from Lyotard's attempts to move away from Freud in the early 1970s; and from Foucault's critical relation to psychoanalysis, notably in *Madness and Civilisation*).

This wariness of a full acceptance of Freudian theories lies in his overly strong characterization of drives and its focus on family relations and infantile sexuality, aspects that Kristeva adopts, for example, in terms of castration and separation from the mother. This opposition mirrors other criticisms of Freud and Lacan, for example, in terms of the scientific basis of their theories and in terms of the highly speculative nature of their work on drives and sexuality. From both critical approaches to psychoanalysis, it follows at least that Kristeva's work is open to the same criticisms as Freud and Lacan.

There are two strong responses to these criticisms and problems. The first is that the deduction of the semiotic is not dependent on psychoanalytic practice in Kristeva's work. Instead, it follows from critical and psychoanalytic study of linguistic theories and the study of works of literature. The validity of Kristeva's studies depends on the strength of her literary and linguistic work, rather than on a secondary authority taken from Freud and Lacan. Indeed, it could be claimed that, if successful, it is possible to follow psychoanalysis in terms of its positing of primary drives without having to follow psychoanalytic practice.

The second response is that Kristeva's work is critical of Freud and Lacan where their work fails to leave a space for an open dialectics that can challenge any given fixed view of drives. This explains why Kristeva combines psychoanalytic theory with critical work on Hegel and with a sense of the importance of ongoing revolution requiring a dialectics, rather than a settled theory of drives and of their role within the subject, society and politics.

Kristeva stresses the dialectical and open (heteronymous) aspects of Freud's theory on drives against tendencies that would wish to naturalize it:

> Post-Freudian theories of drives insist more on the neural-biological aspect of the drive and, in our opinion, accentuate above all the division inherent in the movement of drives. They fail to give similar accent to Freud's fundamental move in seeing a heterogeneity in drives – a signifying and signifiable materiality, conflict-like, and whose successive shocks produce the signifying function through moment of jumping, rupture, separation and absence.   (RPL: 152, my translation)

Kristeva's appeal to drives is not based on biology. One of the reasons for this is that this view fixes drives and sets them up in opposition to one another. A scientific theory of opposed natural drives or instincts is not the basis for Kristeva's work. Instead, she stresses their heterogeneity, that is, their resistance to identification (as if we could speak of this or that natural drive).

Drives are motion, not only in terms of impelling us to motion, but internally, that is, in terms of alterations within the drive and in relation to others. That motion generates meaning, in the sense that it is open to a secondary restriction that allows meaning to emerge. It can be interpreted, but only in a temporary and passing manner, because we never capture the drive. The drives' passage into meaning and structure is a jump, rather than an accurate representation or identification. We never grasp the drives and their conflicts, only their effects and only with the proviso that these effects are changing with the drives in ways that we cannot predict or represent. The semiotic chora is an open field, rather than a fixed explanatory structure.

The symbolic is this restriction, interpretation and assigning of meaning based on drives. It follows from the necessary process of fixing of the semiotic that Kristeva calls the "thetic":

> We shall call this break, which produces the positing of signi-
> fication, a thetic phase. All enunciation, whether of a word or
> of a sentence, is thetic. It requires an identification; in other
> words, the subject must separate from and through his image,
> from and through his objects.   (RPL: 42)

For sense and selves to emerge there has to be a process that imposes an order on the semiotic *chora*. The process of ordering depends upon an assigning of identity.

This assigning is explained by Kristeva in terms of language, and in terms of psychoanalysis and infantile development. Sense requires reference to objects and to subjects. It requires identification of differences and similarities in terms of language itself (words, sentences), in terms of its referents (objects) and in terms of its users (subjects). Similarly, the child evolves out of a semiotic state of many heterogeneous and chaotic drives, into a sense of self and of identity as an active subject, by identifying itself and its surroundings, breaking with its undifferentiated relation to the mother and restricting the variety of drives into meaningful functions.

This work on the child, mother and castration (the break with the mother) is problematic since it appears to restrict the way in which

the semiotic chora can be organized, what it consists of, and our interpretations of it. These Lacanian roots of Kristeva's work are not only
troubling to the extent that they might be false, but also because they
seem to contradict the openness attributed to Freud. For example, the
following passage shows a deep dependence on a notion of castration
that has been widely criticized as a fundamental claim about development "Castration puts the finishing touches on the process of separation
that posits the subject as signifiable, which is to say, separate, always
confronted by another" (RPL: 47). The question is why is it necessary
to define the thetic process in terms of castration, rather than in terms
of a necessary break that can take many forms?

The thetic process gives rise to the symbolic realm, that is, a structure
of signs and rules that permits communication. This realm is deliberately broad in Kristeva's study, because it is designed to include all claims
to well-ordered language (not all possible claims, but all major current
ones). The symbolic is therefore defined, first, as a system connecting
referents (objects referred to), the signified (the meanings associated
to the referent) and signifiers (the perceived things that allow for reference and sense). Secondly, it is defined as presupposing subjects and the
social, that is, the users of language and the context in which referent,
signified and signifier become connected.

Kristeva's main claim about the symbolic realm and its relation to the
semiotic *chora* explains her important position within poststructuralism. She positions structuralist works within the symbolic. This allows
her to criticize them as missing the underlying semiotic processes in two
ways. First, they miss the way the symbolic is negation of the semiotic
(through the thetic processes outlined above). Secondly, they miss the
disruptive, energizing and transformative roles of the semiotic within
the symbolic.

The symbolic is open to revolution and transformation through the
introduction of new unconscious processes into it. This introduction is
both a disruption of current order and the demand for the restriction
of that order through new thetic processes. Here is one of Kristeva's
descriptions of this two-way process in the context of art:

> "Art," on the other hand, by definition does not relinquish the
> thetic even when pulverizing it through the negativity of trans-
> gression. Indeed, this is the only means of transgressing the
> thetic, and the difficulty of maintaining the symbolic function
> under the assault of negativity indicates the risk that textual
> practice represents for the subject. (RPL: 69)

The symbolic realm is transgressed through poetic revolution, that is, its order is challenged through creative forms that negate it (in many different ways charted at length by Kristeva, see "Process in texts: transforming the subject and structure", p. 148). *But this negation itself depends on the move to the symbolic; that is why it is defined in terms of a negation.*

This passage also allows for a further reaction to the critique of Kristeva' work on castration. Her insistence through the book that her analyses focus on texts and textual practice show again that she is not making claims for "natural human drives". Rather, her work is a positing of conditions for language and for the relation between language and poetic creation. She shows how this relation has effects for the subject in language, rather than making the familiar, although much more problematic claim that psychoanalysis on human subjects shows us how language must work.

Critical encounters: poststructuralism and linguistics

A key consequence of Kristeva's work on the dialectics, or interaction through transformations and negations, of the semiotic and the symbolic is her critical survey of a series of linguistic theories. It is through studies of these theories that she is able to come to a definition of the symbolic. These studies are critical, since each one shows how a given aspect of the symbolic is restricted or insufficient.

In terms of poststructuralism and linguistics, Kristeva's arguments are important because they allow poststructuralist linguistics to be situated within contemporary linguistics through a series of carefully argued critical points. In this section, we shall look at aspects of her arguments against Husserl (phenomenological linguistics) and Chomsky (linguistics of deep structure). In the next section, we shall look at Frege (analytic philosophy of language) and Lévi-Strauss (structuralist linguistics). In each case, possible criticisms of Kristeva's position will also be highlighted.

Kristeva's work on Husserl centres on the notion of the transcendental subject, that is, on the question of whether language presupposes the subject as a necessary condition. It is important to stress that the transcendental subject has very little to do with the empirical subject or self. Kristeva is not addressing the point that language requires active speakers, or that it is organized around the notion of a human self (for example, in terms of narrative, or in terms of the positions of addressee and addressor). Instead, the transcendental subject is a condition for language in terms of its directedness for a consciousness, in other words, that it presupposes an "intentional transcendental ego" (RPL: 31). This subject is not an empirical subject (a person) who uses language with all its human aspects and qualities. It is a pared-down consciousness directed towards the world intentionally in its use of language. This is prior to self-hood or character in language; it a is a condition for them.

The transcendental subject is potentially a source for a serious criticism of Kristeva's appeal to the semiotic and to drives. This is because it advocates a condition for language inconsistent with the appeal to drives. In effect, any reflection on drives, any drive considered in language, would presuppose the transcendental subject. This presupposition would not be of the dialectical form advocated by Kristeva, where semiotic drives and the symbolic subject are caught in processes of negation and transformation. Instead, it would set up parts of language as immune to the semiotic and to the poetic revolution. The subject would be prior.

Kristeva's response is to show that the transcendental subject is really only an imposed ordering of prior drives and therefore of the semiotic chora. In the terminology outlined in the previous section, Husserl's transcendental would not be a necessary condition, but a thetic process. As such it would be a contingent and changeable form. In short, the argument is that language does not necessarily require an intentional consciousness.

The argument depends on two important steps. First, Kristeva argues that Husserl's transcendental deduction depends on more than it may appear; this is because it draws up a distinction between the transcendental subject and a sphere that lies outside it but that it is the condition for. Secondly, she points out that this sphere has to be defined in a very strict way for the deduction to hold: a distinction needs to be drawn up between the subject and the sphere of objects.

In turn, these moves allow for the claim that the process of negation that Kristeva situates in the relation between the semiotic and the symbolic holds between the object and the transcendental subject. But it holds twice, in the imposition of a form on the object and on the subject in relation to the object. So Husserl's phenomenology can be seen as a thetic process that illegitimately denies its condition in the semiotic and symbolic relation:

> Therefore, shouldn't the question be what the "I" produces rather than the operations of that "I"? Far from positing the judging "I" as origin, for us such a question merely places the

> thetic and doxic *within the signifying process* that goes beyond
> them, and it raises a new question: How is the thetic, which is
> a positing of the subject, produced? (RPL: 36)

The distinction drawn between production and operation is important because it shows how the subject is related to external processes,
rather than defining necessary conditions from its necessary essence
(its internal operations).

These processes are themselves not produced by the subject, but
producing of the subject. This is why it is not an origin but a consequence of a signifying process, that is, the process that allows language
to make sense and set up relations between a sense and reference. The
doxic, for Kristeva, is the process that allows for a set of beliefs to be
produced (for example, about the nature of objects).

The thetic and the doxic presupposed by Husserl's false origin require
an appeal to something that is not conditioned by the transcendental
subject:

> Previous to the ego thinking within a proposition, no meaning
> exists, but there *do* exist articulations heterogeneous to signifi-
> cation and to the sign: the semiotic *chora*. Though discrete and
> disposed, the *chora* cannot be unified by a Meaning, which, by
> contrast, is unified by a thesis, constituting, as we shall see, a
> break. (RPL: 36)

In mistaking the subject for an origin, that is, for the only condition for
meaning, Husserl misses other conditions that show that the subject is
not an origin. In making this point, Kristeva rejoins other poststructuralists in their critique of the origin (notably, Derrida and Foucault).

However, her methods are very different. Kristeva's deep theoretical commitments make her reading of Husserl, although careful and
backed up by textual evidence, somewhat violent in imposing a vocabulary that Husserl is very careful to avoid (for example, in terms of the
object). This opens up the possibility of a counter to Kristeva through
the point that Husserl's phenomenological reduction (the bracketing
that allows the conditions of thought to emerge) does not make the
distinctions she claims for it. It suspends them, rather than depends
upon them.

This is an important point because Kristeva connects her criticism
of Husserl to her criticism of Chomsky and his claims for a linguistics
based on deep structure. She points out, as many others have, that the

deep grammatical structures deduced by Chomsky are dependent upon a universal and rationalist subject (the "I" in Husserl and Descartes) in a way that shows that the structures cannot be universal, that is, valid for all languages. This is because the subject is not in fact universal, but a contingent and produced form.

For Chomsky, language is separated into a surface structure, an infinite set of combinations of words that we can manipulate into highly complex sentences, and deep structure, a much more restricted set of grammatical rules that governs the creation of valid sentences in the surface structure. Chomsky's theory allows language to be seen as a formal structure despite its apparent complexity, because, however complicated the surface looks, it must have been generated according to the deep rules. Moreover, this allows claims to universal deep structures valid for all languages.

This theory of linguistics would completely invalidate Kristeva's claims because her view that language is open in terms of its transformations cannot allow for universal underlying logical rules. These would restrict poetic revolution, since it could not operate in contravention of the deep grammatical rules. This does not mean that Kristeva is necessarily more radical than Chomsky, since the issue is whether one or the other has the right linguistics.

If Chomsky's theory is true, then it is the right basis for radical critique and for universal claims. Indeed, Chomsky's commitment to the deduction of deep structure on a scientific basis, his rationalism and his belief in the universal communicability of truths, are the basis for a series of strong criticisms of some poststructuralist claims. However, this not in the tired sense of what is clear or difficult, dealt with here in the conclusion to Chapter 2. It is in the sense of universal rules that show different poststructuralist ideas to involve ill-formed or invalid claims.

The originality of Kristeva's counter-claim is that no deep structure can account for the radical transformations in language explicable in terms of the extra-linguistic processes associated with drives:

> We shall see that when the speaking subject is no longer considered a phenomenological transcendental ego nor the Cartesian ego but rather a subject in process/on trial [*sujet en process*], as is the case in the practice of the text, deep structure or at least transformational rules are disturbed and, with them, the possibility of semantic and/or grammatical categorical interpretation. (RPL: 37)

The key term here is "the practice of the text". Kristeva's point is that claims about deep structure must be deduced despite textual creativity (the new ways of writing) and effectiveness (their emotional effect, the need to change rules to take account of them, their capacity to harness drives). In other words, significant combinations in the surface language, in poetry, run counter to the rules defined by deep structure. The revolution in language "works" despite deep structure. So a different explanation must be turned to, that is, one that situates deep structure within the realm of the symbolic (on the surface) and in a dialectical relation with a different kind of depth: unconscious drives and the semiotic *chora* (as defined in the previous section).

According to Kristeva, Chomsky's deduction of the deep structure is only possible if the subject is already presupposed, that is, if language is supposed to function only in terms of actions and an understanding consistent with a specific model of the subject. But if the subject is posited as being an effect of language rather than a condition, it cannot stand as a premise for its own condition in deep structure. The subject is created and transformed. It is related to much wider and more open processes. It cannot be the basis for the deduction of deep universal logical rules.

In order to take these critical oppositions further, it is important to move on to Kristeva' study of texts to see whether it the case that the subject can be sundered in the way she claims. It is in this context that it will also be possible to consider her critical points against Frege's philosophy of language and structuralist linguistics.

Process in texts: transforming the subject and structure

Kristeva's arguments against Frege are similar to her points against Husserl. She claims that the positions of sense and reference (denotation) in language are products of the imposition of a rule, rather than the discovery of a necessary form. Sense and reference are the products of a thetic process that restricts the possibilities of language in relation to prior drives: "We may conclude, therefore, that the thetic is the precondition for both enunciation and denotation" (RPL: 53).

In this case the imposed rule lies in the split between sense and reference, that is, in claiming that any sense depends on the positing of something outside it: in the object. Kristeva claims that even in considering meaning in art, where there is no objective referent, Frege's philosophy of language still depends on the sense–reference distinction, through the *possibility* of reference:

The specific status of signification in art thus results from the constantly maintained ambiguity between the possibility of a meaning that amounts to grammaticality and a denotation that is, likewise, given in the very structure of the judgement or proposition but is realized only under certain conditions ...

(RPL: 53)

Although an artwork may not refer to an actual object, its construction is meant to, at least, indicate the possibility of such a reference, for example, when we consider a possible fictional character.

Against this view of the necessity of reference and of the sense–reference distinction, Kristeva defines literature as a creative mimesis, that is, as the creation of linguistic forms that imitate sense and reference, but distort and undermine their relation. For example, for Frege, truth is the correspondence of a sense with a real object (the cat is on the mat). But in mimesis we only encounter a semblance of the kind of meaning that allows for truth and for a denoting or referring function (thekatiesonthemattress). The key here lies in notions of distortion and subversion. Through mimesis, literature introduces a distortion of grammatical forms and a subversion of underlying symbolic rules (such as sense and reference). It does not deny them as such, but denies their inviolability, introducing a new set of questions as to the conditions for creative production in language.

This subversion extends to the ways of deciding on truth and the presumption of forms of rational subject as valid enunciators (the presumed addressor of a given statement):

> In imitating the constitution of the symbolic as meaning, poetic mimesis is led to dissolve not only the denotative function but also the specifically thetic function of positing the subject. In this respect, modern poetic language goes further than any classical mimesis – whether theatrical or novelistic – because it attacks not only the denotation (the positing of the object) but meaning (the positing of the enunciating subject as well).
>
> (RPL: 58)

So reference fails with the poetic distortion of language, but so does the presumption of a rational, planning subject attempting to convey a specific meaning.

Instead, language is seen as produced, but not necessarily with the intent of communicating a sense. In classical art meanings were produced with no possible real referent, but with modern art even meanings and the assumption of the controlling presence of a rational author fail. The distortion of grammar and of linguistic rules is such that other producers of language enter into the artistic process, or are revealed for the first time (for example, chance is introduced into the writing process).

However, this turn to mimesis emphasizes the possibility of a series of difficult counters to Kristeva. The line of argument is as follows. It does not matter whether language can be distorted. What matters is whether that distortion has any validity or interest. So it is true that grammar can be broken, but what is produced is nonsense, rather than a challenge to reference. A distorted sentence is not a subversion of sense and reference. It is a simple failure that proves the necessity of the rules it breaks. Cannot ungrammaticality simply be discounted as irrelevant to questions of sense, reference and truth?

Similarly, an artwork that is produced under the influence of drugs, or with a high degree of chance, or in common with others, or demanding very great reader input, is not at all a break with a subject. It is a production by a subject under the influence of narcotics, or with other subjects, or with a high degree of chance, or with a great deal of ambiguity requiring interpretation. The necessity of the subject is not questioned at all, only the form and degree of control exercised over the work. Is not the subject always necessary and prior to any other processes that may be introduced into the artwork?

Kristeva's answers to these points turn on the claim that there is meaning in the mimesis of modern art. However, this meaning is not of a well-determined form, in the sense of a fixed meaning that could be associated with a particular object. Instead, the meaning lies in the relation between semiotic drives (the desires associated with a given set of marks) and the disturbance of rules. Indeed, the shock at the absence of easily recognized sense, is a form of meaning for Kristeva.

For instance, when Mallarmé breaks phrases across series of pages, there is both the desire to recombine the separated words into a sentence that makes sense and the desire to linger on the independent words. Moreover, when the broken phrase is itself ambiguous, it brings together a series of possible meanings without allowing any one to dominate or any one to be discarded. We do not have nonsense, since something significant is happening, both to our relation to linguistic rules, and to the relation of our desires to language. Similarly, we do not lose the subject completely in modern poetic creation. We find the subject caught in and produced by a series of processes. So, when Kristeva is criticized for failing to see that the subject is still present, her response is to accept this point, but to deny that the subject can be separated out of a wider series of processes. These processes rest on unconscious drives and desires that connect them and that feed into their transformation: "The subject never is. The *subject* is only the *signifying process* and he appears only as a *signifying practice*, that is, only when he is absent *within the position* out of which social, historical, and signifying activity unfolds" (RPL: 215).

This definition of the subject as processes caught in the dialectical relation of the semiotic and the symbolic – and therefore also part of the thetic process of the necessary imposition of order in language – leads into Kristeva's critique of structuralism. This is because she sees structural analysis as always failing to capture the underlying processes at work behind the structures that they discover. This would not be serious if the structures were independent of the processes that gave rise to them. However, this is not the case.

For example, Kristeva studies the distinction drawn between totemism and sacrifice in the structuralist Lévi-Strauss's work. Totemism involves setting boundaries that cannot be crossed between different forms of life (animals, men and gods, for example – all valued in their own way, but independently and without comparison). Sacrifice, on the contrary, sets the forms up as substitutable (the sacrificed animal, substitutes for man, in an act where a man substitutes for a god). So a language based on totemism should be radically different from one based on sacrifice, because the former must not allow substitutability between symbols, whereas the latter must. But Kristeva points out that totemism emerges out of a sacrifice, in the set of drives and desires negated for the fixed order to emerge. So totemism is a commitment to a symbolic order that denies or forgets the violence and negation that have had to take place for a symbolic order to emerge with the semiotic *chora*. For instance, a totemism based on the absolute separation between two sexes, can only emerge against the background of the sacrifice of desires associated with a third sex or with a crossing of the boundaries between the two sexes (as shown in Chapter 5).

Sacrifice, on the other hand, overemphasizes a particular thetic process that breaks a series of relations into particular separate rules and symbols. Instead of admitting that many different rules could be imposed on primary drives, sacrifice is a "theologization" of the thetic process, because one imposition of rules over a connection of drives is celebrated. The emergence out of disorder is not hidden, but it is fixed both in terms of what rules should emerge and what can legitimately stand as a sacrifice for a wider order: "sacrifice reminds us that the symbolic emerges out of material continuity through a violent and unmotivated leap; whereas totemism is already an appropriation of the continuum based on the symbolic that has already been set in place" (RPL: 78).

The fact that structuralism could not recognize this connection of totemism and sacrifice and their different takes on the semiotic and symbolic relation leads to a far-reaching criticism. Kristeva is able to point out that structuralism cannot criticize totemism for its imposition of a particular order of fixed symbolic distinctions: the order "just is". Nor can it criticize sacrifice for its elevation of a single process of emergence from drives to order: the single process "just is".

Revolution in and through poetry are possible because of a deeper dialectic that relates deep extra-linguistic processes and symbolic orders, but that fixes none:

> Ultimately, such a dialectic lets us view signifying practices as asymmetrically divided – neither absolutising the thetic into a possible theological prohibition, nor negating the thetic in the fantasy of a pulverising irrationalism: neither intransgressable and guilt-producing divine fiat nor "romantic" folly, pure madness, surrealist automatism, or pagan pluralism. Instead, we see the condition of the subject of significance as a heterogeneous contradiction between two irreconcilable elements – separate but inseparable from the process in which they assume asymmetrical functions. (RPL: 82)

Kristeva's poststructural revolution in poetic language resists claims to universal laws and to natural symbolic orders. But it also resists nihilistic claims to unreason and chaos. Instead, the relation of our drives to our languages becomes the site for a critical revolution that overturns the false subordination of language to deep rules and logics, and the attendant social and political subordinations that insinuate themselves under the cover of this "necessity" or "nature".

seven

Conclusion: poststructuralism into the future

A new enlightenment

Poststructuralism has an important role to play in a new enlightenment. A fresh movement is required to restore the role of creative and critical thought in all aspects of life. Poststructuralist works excel in this critical function due to their varied, rigorous and deep questioning of traditions and structures. But their role is not solely negative. They also stand out in the multiple ways in which they redefine creativity in relation to a creative staleness and lack of impact. Radical critique and creativity go hand in hand. In relation to them, thought becomes more mobile and flexible. It thereby also becomes a greater force for change.

Since its beginnings in the eighteenth century, enlightenment, or the use of reason in knowledge, ethics and the arts, has had constructive and destructive roles, although both must be seen as positive in the fight against the enemies of deep thought. Destructively, enlightenment defends thought against all forms of dogmatism (the belief in unexamined or false ideas and values). It also defends life against the absence of critical and creative thought, that is, against inertia and stupidity. Finally, it fights against the misuse of thought in a deliberate defence or spreading of falsehoods, for example, in a pandering to ungrounded fears for personal gain or power.

Positively, enlightenment contributes to the construction of open ways of life based on critical thought. To do this it contributes to the creation of ideas that foster forms of life resistant to negative influences such as dogmatism and the self-interested preservation of false ideas.

With poststructuralist thought, openness is taken to a very high level through a constant commitment to difference: how can lives and societies remain open to that which differs from them?

Wherever sameness and identity are taken as foundations, poststructuralism uncovers concealed differences. It seeks to affirm these differences in response to illegitimate exclusions and, thereby, it extends and transforms enlightened rationality. Thought – an extension of the use of reason from the earlier age of enlightenment – is turned to the external borders of forms of knowledge. These borders are shown to be at work even within the powers that exclude them: the limits of knowledge are at work in positive ways at its core.

Poststructuralism and enlightenment are about the formulation of questions, of methods and of principles that reveal the difficult problems that thought has to struggle with. If it is to be genuinely open, thought must not turn away from these problems. The questions, methods and principles provide a framework for the creation of ideas and concepts that transform problems in order to alter their negative hold on life.

This must be done without hiding that grip, or pretending that it can disappear once and for all. Only dogmatism promises such miracles in any part of life. This is the first reason why much of the openness and rationality of current societies is merely apparent, missing the real problems at work. The difficulty of poststructuralist works is not a whimsical or dishonest decision to make simple truths obscure. It is a careful attempt to show the complexity of reality and of the problems that beset life. It is also, though, an affirmation of the rich differences that can enhance life.

Against these definitions, it could be argued that enlightenment is foremost a struggle against cruelty and evil. But, although important, this struggle is not the primary function of enlightenment. Some cruelty results from ignorance, for example, from superstition, but not all. Evil is a word with stronger roots in dogmatism than in enlightenment, since it provides the illusion of an explanation, where there is only the lazy or disingenuous recourse to prior and often unexamined values. Evil is a label used out of lack of understanding.

Poststructuralism and enlightenment cannot have the struggle against cruelty and evil as their main functions. These only follow from a prior commitment to thought. The struggle against ignorance can work against cruelty and injustice. Greater thoughtfulness can allow for a movement away from definitions of evil and towards the understanding of cruelty and violence. But the main thrust of thought must be against ignorance and stupidity. In terms of these struggles, it is important to realize that cruelty and violence are possible within thought itself, in unchecked ideas, or in methods applied without sensitivity, or in principles lacking balances, or in the many powerful forms of self-deception.

For example, Deleuze argues that if recognition is taken as a key faculty in thought, then it will have been set up as conservative from the start. This is because the model of recognition presupposes a prior familiarity and defines thought against radical experiences from the very beginning. He argues that this is a false model for thought, notably because there is no first representation to start from. In this, he rejoins Derrida and Foucault's criticism of origins. There is no pure origin; it always has deeper roots and it changes with what follows it.

With poststructuralism, enlightenment has added resources in the critique of the hold of the faculty of recognition on thought and of its capacity to bolster conservatism. Poststructuralist thinkers deploy many different critiques of the origin against false claims to pure beginnings and values that are external to the contingencies and variations of history. Pure values and pure sources are forms of dogmatism. They are the basis for illegitimate exclusions; for example, in terms of judgements regarding fallen forms of life that are supposed to betray the origin and its purity. There are no such fallen forms. There was nowhere to fall from.

Again, against this alliance of enlightenment and poststructuralism, it could be remarked that the critical and creative resources of thought are already in place, but that we lack the will or capacity to put them into practice. It could then be claimed that poststructuralism is one such obstacle, both sapping the will and obfuscating real values. The first point misses the dynamic nature of the problems and responses at stake. The form of any enlightenment must change, as reason and life change, according to the dominant forces and demands at work within them. The nature of power, technology, capital and what we understand human life and all of life to be have all changed over the last centuries. These changes demand different responses in terms of resistance, adaptation and the exploration of the benefits that may flow from them.

Poststructuralism is, then, neither cause for loss of will, nor cause for confusion. It highlights new relations between thought and its contexts. It explains the relation between thought and society, life and often unconscious conditions. These explanations demand new ways of thinking about the role and revolutionary power of reason and of thought. They are grounds not for despair, but for renewed enthusiasm. They are not difficult to the point of confusion, but exciting additions to knowledge and powerful transformations of it.

Poststructuralism and enlightenment: critical counters

Each of the poststructuralist works studied here provides new answers to the limitations faced by the enlightenment project in modern times. Each also outlines new ways of thinking about the difficulties faced by thought, both from within and externally. Foucault demonstrates how power has evolved in relation to new ways of thinking about the subject and about human freedom. In reaction to these changes, he suggests new ways of thinking about history and about the relation between subjects, knowledge and events. Deleuze shows how common sense and judgement are still indebted to metaphysical commitments to identity and to representation, to the detriment of more valuable senses of differences and variations in repetition.

Derrida shows the negative metaphysical presuppositions at work in even the most rational and well-meaning texts. He gives us a wide variety of textual techniques and practical cases to extend to new ways of thinking about truth and its positive and negative relations to violence. Lyotard reminds us of events that lie beyond the boundaries of reason and yet that matter, if we are to claim to be just in responding to irresolvable conflicts. Kristeva shows how each novel way of thinking about language and the revolutionary power of art must take account of unconscious processes at work, before any determined form of language comes into play.

None of these thinkers advocates an abandonment of reason or of thought. Rather, each suggests ways of refining thought in practical situations on the basis of new and more subtle and inclusive definitions. They do not advocate a rejection of the positive thrust of enlightenment, but a careful and rigorous critical and creative work to maintain its power and to thwart its capacity for self-destruction and its tendency to stasis.

It is possible to think of this relation between reason and thought in a new enlightenment as a dialogue or dialectic between reason and what stands outside it. Each transforms and informs the other and neither can stand alone. This comes out strongly in the refusal of poststructuralist authors to take up absolutely "anti" positions, in particular, anti-science. Instead, the main question is how to preserve science from becoming a falsely exclusive arbiter of truth, while maintaining its capacity to open new fields for knowledge and to defend life against ignorance.

Science performs a central role in enlightenment through its capacity to debunk superstition and forms of dogmatism in their far remove from evidence and consistency. It is also crucial to hope in the future through its capacity to revolutionize our practical lives and infuse them with deep understanding of our environment and our place within it. Science is a source of both the harsh refusal of ignorance and the delight in life characteristic of rational enlightenment. If poststructuralism were anti-science – as has sometimes been claimed – then there would be no sense in its association with enlightenment. But, as shown in each of the previous chapters, it is not anti-science. Poststructuralism has a critical relation to science, not in order to eliminate it, but to allow it to thrive, without itself turning into a force that denies its own reforming and open character. Poststructuralism also has a creative relation to science, in terms of its relation to extra-scientific forms of thought, for example, in the arts or in relation to history and to ethics. Science is central to any enlightenment, but only in harness with others sources of ideas and truth that subject it to criticism and to external influence. There is no pure science and science cannot be the final arbiter of truth.

Yet, two further objections must be answered in making this claim for the future of thought and of poststructuralism. Why would a movement return to the idea of enlightenment, when many of its critical arguments seem to apply to enlightenment values and principles? Why would any enlightenment turn to poststructuralist thought, when it has satisfactory values of its own, indeed, when these values sometimes seem inconsistent with those of poststructuralism? Is not poststructuralism anti-enlightenment (despite claims for dialogue)? Does this not mean that it can have no role to play except outside that tradition?

Such questions miss a key aspect of poststructuralism. It works within what it follows, not in order to destroy it in the name of something better and different, but in order to bring out its greatest capacity for openness to change in line with its highest values. This openness is political. It is an invitation to experiment with new ways of thinking about difference and about the limits of knowledge. It is also a challenge to all ways of thinking in terms of fixed values and identities. Nothing is ever the same through time or within its spatial limits, and when we cling to the illusion of such sameness we impose the values of a false identity on what differs from it.

This relation to a guiding identity is one of the greatest problems for enlightenment. How is it to construct and use rational ideas, without clinging to forms of reason that exclude forms of life or fail to be flexible in relation to new obstacles? How is it to remain critical of its own tendencies to sameness and stasis, when it must also remain vigilant against its enemies in conservatism, self-interest and ignorance, or an alliance of all three? How is it to fight against its own necessary tendency to particular roots, when the power of unrestrained markets and technology, as well as resurgent old dogmatic enemies, seems to demand an uncompromising commitment to reason?

All the authors studied here work with these challenges in mind. They are not nihilists and it is a mistake to confuse the radical critique of certain forms of reason with an opposition to the value of thought. However, it is also a mistake to assume that an enlightenment constructed around reason and guided by secure values can escape poststructuralist criticisms. It is not that rational scrutiny, scientific discovery and enquiry, and the values of tolerance, humanism and democracy must be discarded. It is that they should be sometimes added to, sometimes taken further, and sometimes tempered.

For example, Lyotard's work on differences that cannot be bridged is not anti-democratic. Rather, he wants to encourage thought about the kinds of situation where democratic decisions may still be unjust. He also wants to suggest forms of ethics and appeals to feelings that help us to testify to events that reveal this injustice. Finally, he believes that democracy must evolve with an awareness of its historical roots and of their dependence on forms of narrative that define insiders and outsiders (if only because democracy is founded by a few in the name of many). This is not to oppose democracy, but to set out the conditions for its extension.

This work cannot take place from within an enlightenment or rationalist orthodoxy. Any such appeal to a consistent core would miss the necessary flexibility demanded by the critical and self-critical qualities of enlightenment. It would also miss the creativity necessary for the transformation of thought in line with changes in life and society; as these evolve, so must thought. This is not to play down the force of an appeal to a commitment to orthodoxy in difficult times. Rather, it is to claim that this appeal leads to a counter-productive position where the deepest values of enlightenment are discarded in favour of its own inner tendency to dogmatism.

This tendency explains the poststructuralist critique of enlightenment. It is not a full rejection, but an awareness of violent exclusions, mistaken certainties and strategic errors. For example, a restrictive definition of thought that overemphasizes rationality excludes aspects of thought that are both important and impossible to eliminate. Poststructuralism charts forms that resist incorporation into rationality, such as feelings or the unconscious. It does not merely do so in order to show a rejection or an incompatibility, but to argue that feelings and the unconscious are present even in the rationality that rejects them.

Kristeva argues that any language or symbolic system presupposes a set of unconscious extra-linguistic processes. Systems must involve these processes in terms of what is rejected and what is cut out from prior material movements and impulses when the basic structure of the language are instituted; for example, in the way a labelling system allows some things to appear and sets up a relation between labels and things, while missing other impulses and movements that fail to be labelled or that go beyond the limits of the identified things. Language does not allow us to see everything that is there. It negates some things in favour of others, not only in terms of objects, but in terms of how language itself is supposed to work and fail.

The underlying processes are the rejections, negations and valuations that allow for a systematic language to emerge. But any language also contains the seeds of its own disturbance and destruction, in the revolutionary potential of poetic language. The value of what some may judge to be poetic nonsense or delirium lies in the challenge that can be mounted against any apparent naturalness of a system; for example, that we must think in terms of subjects and successful acts, or in terms of a dominant set of truths and values. Value and truth are also in the revelation of a hidden potential for any language to be different and to evolve. Enlightenment should not fear revolution. Neither should it pre-judge what can stand as revolution.

To miss this complicated interrelation of the body and the mind, of feelings and deductions, of consciousness and the unconscious, of the known and the new is therefore to fall back on false certainties, for example, on the free and autonomous human subject, or on a notion of pure rationality. This a strategic mistake, since it cuts off an important source of knowledge and strength, while also overestimating the actual strength and resistance of, for example, free choice or individual rational calculations. They are more fragile than they might seem and to ignore that inner fragility is to weaken them further. They can be made stronger, but only when distilled with what appears external and foreign to them. But is not this turn to complexity false on two counts? First, if difficult problems are to be overcome it is by simplifying them. It is not enough to claim that this simplification is wrong, if it is the only way forwards. Secondly, even if it is accepted that there is a necessary relation between different things, this does not mean that they have the same value.

Against poststructuralism, the point of enlightenment could therefore be to disentangle different forms of life and thought, in order to allow us to act on the higher values and against lower ones. With its emphasis on synthesis, rather than on a simplifying analysis, and with its dependence on notions of infinite connection, rather than division, poststructuralism appears to be destined to be hopelessly impractical and incapable of differentiating high and low values. But this is not the case; complexity can lead to effective action and to careful distinctions.

Poststructuralism and pragmatism

Complexity and connection are terms that have recurred throughout this book. In looking beyond the limits of knowledge, and in drawing those limits back into the core, poststructuralist works show how familiar forms are not independent from one another and from what may have appeared distant and strange. However, the poststructuralist response to these intricate connections can seem frustratingly complicated and hard to put into practice. Can there be more simple plans and practical applications?

In one sense, the answer must be no, but this need not be detrimental to poststructural practice, since it follows from an important and productive aspect of a poststructuralist view of reality. Although all things participate in the same world, although they are immanent to that world, this does not mean that they belong to the same levels or categories. Any poststructuralist pragmatism must take account of different relations between things and their conditions. A condition is a not a cause, but rather an influence and something that sets principles or limits.

For example, in addition to relations of cause and effect between things (A causes B to move), a transcendental philosophy can determine relations in terms of principles (A can never be considered to be completely independent of B). Although principles cannot answer certain types of practical questions (Who did this? How do we move that?), they can give guidelines for approaching different kinds of questions (What forms can reality take? What questions are legitimate? Are there any fundamental objects?).

In terms of this kind of distinction, Deleuze allows for important pragmatic principles such as "Real experimentation in the arts must cross the boundaries of identities we take for granted". Independent of whether any given principle is true, it is a least possible to say that thought, when approached in terms of conditions, can provide practical elements to any approach. Indeed, such guidelines have the advantage of not specifying a given action, but leaving this more open to experimentation in line with differing perspectives and situations.

If all things belong to the same level, practice can take the form of working according to more or less simplifying plans and representations. We know to greater or lesser degrees how something works, that is, we have a representation of it. This allows us to try things out and, depending on the accuracy of the plan, to succeed, or to learn from failure. We can then amend the plan and move on.

Poststructuralism rejects this form of pragmatism, of practical philosophy, because it takes the theory of plans or of representations to be false. Where things are conditions for one another, that is, for a transcendental philosophy, there is no relation of representation between them. The conditions are not pictures or models of what they are conditions for, that is, the relations between things in the conditioned realm are not the same as those between the things in the realm of conditions. The two do not mirror one another.

Much of the difficulty of poststructuralist work stems from this asymmetry and from its incompatibility with our familiarity with maps and plans. This does not mean that transcendental philosophy cannot be pragmatic, in the sense of experimenting and learning from creative experimentation. On the contrary, learning is at the heart of most poststructuralist philosophies, for example, in later Foucault, in Deleuze's difference and repetition, in Kristeva's works on writing and learning, in Derrida's works on philosophical education, or in Lyotard's late works on Augustine. However, a poststructuralist pragmatism is much less secure in its ability to separate different parts of experiment or practical knowledge from one another. It is not a matter of revising things piece by piece. They are interconnected and any practical work is a transformation of all of them. Yet some order is still possible because how they are transformed is different, both in terms of the alteration of the parts and their relations, and in terms of spatial and chronological relations. Different realms presuppose different senses of space and time and, therefore, any experiment involves long and short effects, and, more importantly, effects that are, in some sense, outside time in its familiar linear sense.

Asymmetry then becomes an opportunity to describe different functions in each realm. This explains why poststructuralism is a philosophy of principles, limits, critical guidelines and radical creativity. These do not stand outside any experiment. They are open to revision, but in a different way to the revisions in the realms they condition. For example, Foucault's history is both subject to standard rules about objectivity, in collecting objective evidence, and to principles that stem from the continuity of history, in making decisions about what evidence to count in or out. Both limitations must be applied and both can be changed, but how and why they change are different and a change in one does not imply a corresponding one in the other. This does not mean that they have no effects on one another, but that these effects can be very small or very large in one, independent of their scale in another.

Foucault's work therefore allows for many different practical guides and principles depending on which realm is being dealt with. There can be the principle that as many different sources of evidence should be sought out, alongside the condition that a principle for selecting each should be determined. The practice of history is not left vague and open by Foucault. Quite the contrary: it is opened on to a much wider set of practical questions that extend its scope and its powers of scrutiny.

As a crucial part of any enlightenment, the impact of history is changed by poststructuralism. History becomes part of any determination of the practice and values of enlightenment itself. Where once history could have been seen as that which enlightenment sought to escape through a reason and a set of values that did not change historically, it now becomes a key critical function in an open-ended dialectical transformation of enlightenment.

Individuals, poststructuralism and enlightenment

Poststructuralism denies any founding value in common sense. It also denies any theoretical boundaries for pragmatism in terms of its actors and its goals. What is to be achieved, by who and for whom are part of a practice and an experiment. This is because the subject – the human subject, for example – does not count as a secure foundation. Nor do human values (or godly ones) stand independent of context and revision. This denial of independence extends to the judges of success or failure. There is no independent judge and no independent authority to make final decisions about what is to count as a successful social experiment or how a failed one should be reviewed.

Again, this appears to force poststructuralism into an impossible situation. Can it make any sense to speak of a practice, without having a secure sense of the subject of that practice? Can we have pragmatism without goals? Why have a pragmatism if there is no external judge of its evolution? These questions miss a key point about poststructuralist works: they do not deny the subject. Instead, they deny its founding independence. It is possible to work with a notion of the subject and of goals, so long as they are open to critical scrutiny and to experimentation regarding their boundaries. The questions "For whom?", "By who?" and "What for?" are part of poststructuralist enquiry.

The authors studied here demonstrate how the subject can neither be taken as a firm beginning, nor taken as the standard for setting goals. Much wider connections must be taken into account; for example, in terms of networks of power (Foucault), sensual and virtual intensities (Deleuze), feelings that extend beyond the boundaries of knowledge (Lyotard), multiple relations between texts (Derrida) and pre-linguistic impulses and negations (Kristeva). It is possible to speak of the subject and of its goals, but only with great care and with an awareness of their limitations.

These limitations have a critical and creative importance because they allow for much more precise and truthful accounts of the processes we have to work within. We do not only deal with the free decisions of rational subjects, but with much wider forces that cannot be approached in the same way as rational interlocutors. According to poststructuralism, it is not even possible to set such rational standards as a goal, since these limits can be traced to the heart of rationalism and of the human subject, for example, in the remnants of the denial of those limits in the rational search for absolutes, or, in the human unconscious and its role in conscious decisions (think of your dreams when an important and difficult decision looms).

This critical and creative extension to the subject is positive because it allows poststructuralist thinkers to go beyond one of the main paradoxes of enlightenment: the combination of individualism and of a common reason. The human individual and its free rational decisions are, at the same time, crucial to traditional enlightenment in terms of the hope for a better common future and a barrier to that future through the challenge this freedom poses to common rational decisions. If we use the same reason and come to the same decisions, then can we really be called free? If we are free, then is there not something important that goes beyond reason? But if this thing beyond reason draws us apart, for example in terms of our desires, how then is reason to stand as the grounds for a communal progress?

Once the subject and reason are set among wider processes and stripped of any privilege within them, the question of how we can be both free and conditioned by reason loses its difficult edge. With it, we also lose some of the most difficult political problems of enlightenment in terms of the relation between the value of individual choice and the fact of different degrees of freedom associated with background and environment. We are not equally free and we live in systems where that equality is a mirage.

The new challenge is, therefore, not only how to achieve as much equality as possible, but also, and more importantly, how to open up systems so that we at least achieve an equality of inclusion, as opposed to the rejection of those or that which differs. This means subjecting all systems and beliefs to critique with respect to what they reject. It means to subject them to a creative transformation with respect to adapting to radical differences.

A very different set of questions guides poststructuralism when compared to the problems of individualism. What are the structures, systems and processes at work in life? How can these be opened to change and difference? What are the dangers of this openness? What are the dangers in resisting openness? How can openness be fostered best in terms of these dangers? Where should one experiment creatively and where not?

The relation between the acts that follow from these questions and the structures, systems and processes is necessarily an indirect one. There is no direct causal chain going from an absolutely free decision to a given outcome. Instead, different courses of action, guided by principles, must be tried out within a complex situation. We experiment not to find a certain path, but to interact with a situation that changes as we work within it. This is an oblique relation to a situation; like playing against an adaptable partner, rather than with a set of fixed rules to be discovered once and for all.

There is no contradiction in denying freedom yet still claiming to "try something out" because here "to try" indicates a relative looseness in a situation, rather than an absolute free will. We are not completely free to come to a decision; rather, the many different influences on an act allow for thought in terms of decisions. These decisions are themselves influenced, but we can consider them to be relatively free, to the point of thinking of them as our decisions, but only temporarily and always in a manner open to critique and to different creative interpretations.

It would be possible to discover after the fact that we were not free in a given situation. It would be possible to decide for strategic reasons not to act as if we were free. It would be possible to make selections of areas where we decided to act as if free and others where we decided not to. These outcomes would lead not to an outright denial of freedom, but of its adaptation to new environments. This adaptation releases its political capacity to transform life allied to thought.

Poststructuralism is often defined in terms of negative power. It is seen as a movement that takes away options, perhaps as one that takes all of them away, leaving the field open for a return of confusion and dogmatism. But it has never been negative in this way. Poststructuralism is a movement of addition, but where addition means a transformation rather than collection. Added to the spirit of enlightenment, poststructuralism is the most powerful resistance to ignorance and creator of liberating thought available today.

Questions for discussion and revision

one Introduction: what is poststructuralism?

1. What is the common thread running through poststructuralism?
2. What are some of the main criticisms of poststructuralism and how can they be answered?
3. Why is poststructuralism above all a practice?
4. How is poststructuralism a politics of the left?
5. What is the significance of the historical roots of poststructuralism?
6. What is truth for poststructuralist thinkers?
7. Is poststructuralism anti-science?
8. What is the relation of poststructuralism to capitalism, democracy and human rights?

two Poststructuralism as deconstruction: Jacques Derrida's *Of Grammatology*

1. Why is Derrida's work hard to read? What reading strategies are helpful responses to this difficulty?
2. What does Derrida mean by origin, presence, trace, différance, and play? What work do these terms do for deconstructions?
3. How and why is deconstruction a tracing of metaphysical presuppositions in texts?
4. What are some of the main critical points to be made against deconstruction?
5. What is the relation of deconstruction to science?
6. Is Derrida's work unethical, due to its difficulty and to its resistance to ethical absolutes?

three Poststructuralism as philosophy of difference: Gilles Deleuze's *Difference and Repetition*

1. How does the relation of Deleuze's work to structuralism allow for an understanding of his philosophy?
2. Why does Deleuze's poststructuralism go beyond the object and beyond our ideas about the object?
3. What is reciprocal determination and what is its importance?
4. What is Deleuze's definition of problems?
5. How is Deleuze's philosophy a challenge to the founding notion of the subject?
6. What is a simulacrum?
7. Why is poststructuralism not open to the criticisms of postmodernism?
8. What is a sign?
9. What are the practical consequences of Deleuze's definition of thought?

four Poststructuralism as philosophy of the event: Jean-François Lyotard's *Discours, figure*

1. What is the role of feelings and events in Lyotard's poststructuralism?
2. Why does Lyotard oppose totalities and what does Lyotard mean by incommensurability?
3. What is the difference between politics and the political?
4. What is the figural in Lyotard's early work?
5. Does Lyotard oppose any sense of truth?
6. Why do poststructuralists question the distinction drawn between theory and practice?
7. How do poststructuralist ideas challenge our views of cities?
8. What does Lyotard mean by a differend? Can the term have a positive political function?

five Poststructuralism, history, genealogy: Michel Foucault's *The Archaeology of Knowledge*

1. What is the significance of poststructuralism for the study of history?
2. What are the main critical questions to be put to Foucault's account of freedom?
3. What does Foucault mean by continuity and by discontinuity on history?
4. Can accurate definitions be given of genealogy and of archaeology?
5. How is Foucault's poststructuralism a form of critique?
6. How can Foucault's politics be described as progressive?
7. Why is the definition of a statement as a relation so important for Foucault's archaeology?
8. What is the critical contrast between Foucault's archaeology and science?

six Poststructuralism, psychoanalysis, linguistics: Julia Kristeva's *Revolution in Poetic Language*

1. How is Kristeva's poststructuralism revolutionary?
2. How are poetic text and language related?
3. What is the semiotic? What is the symbolic? Why is their relation so important for Kristeva?
4. How does Kristeva's dependence on psychoanalysis lead to criticisms of her work? How can these criticisms be answered?
5. What does Kristeva mean by the thetic? What is its function?
6. How does her poststructuralist linguistics allow for criticisms of phenomenological linguistics?
7. What is Kristeva's criticism of deep structures in linguistics?
8. What is mimesis for Kristeva? How is it associated with the undermining of linguistic rules?

Further reading

All the authors studied here have published a great number of works. An even greater number of secondary texts have been written on them. In order to provide a first guide through this daunting set of books and articles, I have provided suggestions for further reading, as well as the bibliographical details for the primary texts studied here. The point is to give a major work by each author, followed by a more accessible work or collection (a set of interviews or essays, for example) and a strong representative academic collection. In terms of secondary texts, for each author I recommend a general introduction, a critical collection and, for some authors, a harder critical work by a thinker representative of a counter-position. The aim is not to provide a final judgement of primary or secondary texts, but ways into balanced, informed and critical assessments.

Works by and on Jacques Derrida

The major text studied here is *Of Grammatology*, Gayatri Chakravorty Spivak (trans.) (Baltimore, MD: Johns Hopkins University Press, 1974) [*De la grammatologie* (Paris: Minuit, 1967)]. See also "Différance", in *Margins of Philosophy*, A. Bass (trans.), 1–28 (Chicago, IL: University of Chicago Press, 1984) and *Politics of Friendship*, G. Collins (trans.) (London: Verso, 1997). A good collection of works by Derrida is Peggy Kamuf (ed.), *A Derrida Reader: Between the Blinds* (New York: Columbia University Press, 1991). For an introduction to Derrida's work, see Geoffrey Bennington and Jacques Derrida, *Jacques Derrida* (Chicago, IL: University of Chicago Press, 1999). For a definitive collection of critical essays (this is important, because smaller collections do not capture the profusion of different angles on his work) see Len Lawlor and Zeynep Direk (eds), *Derrida: Critical Assessments* (London: Routledge, 2002) [this work is very expensive and is best consulted in libraries, in particular, for the seminal essays by his contemporaries]. For a good and much more affordable critical collection see David Wood (ed.), *Derrida: A Critical Reader* (Oxford: Blackwell, 1992).

Works by and on Gilles Deleuze

The major texts studied here are: *Difference and Repetition*, P. Patton (trans.) (New York: Columbia University Press, 1995) [*Différence et repetition* (Paris: PUF, 1968)]; "How do we Recognize Structuralism?", in *Desert Islands and other Texts (1953–1974)*, M. Taromina (trans.), 170–92 (New York: Semiotext(e), 2003); "What Prisoners want from Us", in *Desert Islands and other Texts*, 204–5; and *Proust and Signs*, R. Howard (trans.) (London: Continuum, 2000). *Desert Islands and other Texts* is also an excellent collection of Deleuze's early works. Readers should also refer to the two deeply influential works with Félix Guattari: *Anti-Oedipus* (Minneapolis, MN: University of Minnesota Press, 1983) and *A Thousand Plateaus* (Minneapolis, MN: University of Minnesota Press, 1987). There are two good general introductions to Deleuze's works: Todd May's *Gilles Deleuze: An Introduction* (Cambridge: Cambridge University Press, 2005) is more philosophical and political; Claire Colebrook's *Gilles Deleuze* (London: Routledge, 2001) is more literary and aesthetic. Paul Patton (ed.), *Gilles Deleuze: A Critical Reader* (Oxford: Blackwell, 1997) is an excellent collection of critical essays. For a counter-position by another major philosopher, I recommend Alain Badiou's *Deleuze: The Clamor of Being* (Minneapolis, MN: University of Minnesota Press, 1999).

Works by and on Jean-François Lyotard

The major work studied here is *Discours, figure* (Paris: Klincksieck, 1971). Other important works are *The Differend: Phrases in Dispute* (Minneapolis, MN: University of Minnesota Press, 1988) and *Libidinal Economy* (London: Athlone Press, 1993). A good collection of Lyotard's works that also includes translations of important parts of *Discours, figure* is Keith Crome and James Williams (eds), *The Lyotard Reader and Guide* (Edinburgh: Edinburgh University Press, 2005). *Jean-François Lyotard* (London: Routledge, 2002) by Simon Malpas is a good general introduction. The best collection of critical essays on Lyotard is in Robert Harvey and Lawrence Schehr (eds), *Yale French Studies, Number 99: Jean-Francois Lyotard: Time and Judgment* (New Haven, CT: Yale University Press, 2001).

Works by and on Michel Foucault

The major work studied here is *The Archaeology of Knowledge*, A. M. Sheridan Smith (trans.) (London: Routledge, 1989) [*L'Archéologie du savoir* (Paris: Gallimard, 1969)]. Paul Rabinow (ed.), *The Foucault Reader* (Harmondsworth: Penguin, 1984) is a good selection of Foucault's works, but readers are encouraged to consult Foucault's other influential main works, for example, *The History of Sexuality: An Introduction* (Harmondsworth: Penguin, 1990) or the important collection *Power/Knowledge* (New York: Pantheon, 1980). Although it is quite difficult, Gilles Deleuze's book on Foucault, *Foucault* (Minneapolis, MN: University of Minnesota Press, 1988), offers wonderful insights into both thinkers. For a more general introduction, see Sarah Mills's *Michel Foucault* (London: Routledge, 2003). For a good collection of critical essays, see David Couzens Hoy (ed.), *Foucault: A Critical Reader* (Oxford: Blackwell, 1986).

Works by and on Julia Kristeva

The major work studied here is abridged as *Revolution in Poetic Language*, Margaret Waller (trans.) (New York: Columbia University Press, 1984) [*La révolution du langage poétique* (Paris: Seuil, 1974)]. For good collections of Kristeva's works see Toril Moi (ed.), *The Kristeva Reader* (New York: Columbia University Press, 1986) or, more up-to-date, Kelly Oliver (ed.), *The Portable Kristeva* (New York: Columbia University Press, 1997). *Black Sun* is one of her most powerful works on psychoanalysis (New York: Columbia University Press, 1992), whereas *Powers of Horror: An Essay on Abjection* (New York: Columbia University Press, 1982) is recommended as a great literary critical work. A comprehensive collection of critical essays is John Lechte and Mary Zournazi (eds), *The Kristeva Critical Reader* (Edinburgh: Edinburgh University Press, 2004). For a study of her work on gender see Sarah Beardsworth, *Julia Kristeva: Psychoanalysis and Modernity* (Albany, NY: SUNY Press, 2004) and for a more general introduction see Noelle McAfee, *Julia Kristeva* (New York: Routledge, 2003).

Publications timeline

This timeline is designed to situate a set of works within an epoch. It should not be read as exhaustive or as an indicator of value, but merely as a preliminary reference point for relating works to one another and to historical events. No such events have been indicated here since the necessarily restricted selection would bias any future readings; for example, for some readers a focus on social events – May 1968 – should be balanced by a focus on wars – Vietnam – and on science – moon landings. For reasons of economy some titles have been cited in short form, and all dates refer to original publication.

	Derrida	Deleuze/Deleuze & Guattari	Lyotard	Foucault	Kristeva	Others
						Lacan: Seminars
1953		• Empiricism and Subjectivity				
1954			• Phenomenology			
1955						
1956			• Essays for Socialism or Barbary			
1961				• Madness and Civilization		
1962		• Nietzsche and Philosophy				
1963		• Kant's Critical Philosophy		• Birth of the Clinic		
1966		• Bergsonism		• The Order of Things		Lacan: Ecrits
1967	• Writing and Difference • Of Grammatology	• Proust and Signs				
1968		• Spinoza et le problème de l'expression [Expressionism in Philosophy] • Difference and Repetition				Serres: Hermes Vol. 1
1969		• The Logic of Sense		• Archaeology of Knowledge	• Semeiotiké	
1970						
1971			• Discours, figure			
1972	• Dissemination • Margins • Positions	• Anti-Oedipus				Serres: Hermes Vol. 2 Kofman: Nietzsche and Metaphor

	Derrida	Deleuze/Deleuze & Guattari	Lyotard	Foucault	Kristeva	Others
1974	• Glas					**Serres**: Hermes Vol. 3 **Irigaray**: Speculum
1975				• Surveiller et punir [Discipline and Punish]		
1976				• History of Sexuality I		
1977	• Limited Inc.				• Polylogue	**Serres**: Hermes Vol. 4 **Irigaray**: This Sex which is not One
1979			• The Postmodern Condition			
1980		• A Thousand Plateaus				**Serres**: Hermes Vol. 5
1981	• The Postcard				• Powers of Horror	
1982						**Irigaray**: Elemental Passions
1983		• Cinema 1	• The Differend			**Nancy**: The Inoperative Community
1984	• Of an Apocalyptic Tone			• History of Sexuality II • History of Sexuality III	• Tales of Love	**Irigaray**: An Ethics of Sexual Difference
1985		• Cinema 2				
1986		• Foucault				
1987	• Of Spirit				• Black Sun	
1988		• The Fold	• The Inhuman		• Strangers to Ourselves	**Badiou**: Being and Event **Nancy**: Experience of Freedom
1990						**Irigaray**: Je, Tu, Nous
1991		• What is Philosophy?	• Lessons on the Analytic of the Sublime			
1993		• Critique and Clinic	• Postmodern Moralities			
1994				• Dits et Ecrits [collected lectures and other works], 1954–88	• New Maladies of the Soul	
1996					• Sense and Non-sense of Revolt	**Nancy**: Being Singular Plural
2000			• Misery of Philosophy			

Index